I fell about laughing at Diz White's book, her hilarious showbiz stories woven into her hunt for a cottage are a hoot... her writing allows you to not only imagine you are there, but to feel you have embraced the heart of the Cotswolds.
A great holiday read or a great read anytime.

— Debbie McGee
***BBC** Radio Berkshire's 'The Debbie McGee Show'*

The ultimate, laugh-out-loud, foodie, good life, house-hunting, travel-tour, meet the locals, fun read. If you are holding *COTSWOLDS MEMOIR* in your hands you are a lucky person.

— Wanda Ventham
Actress and Cotswolds resident,
Midsomer Murders, The Lotus Eaters, Dr.Who

Diz White has presented us with a souvenir of the Cotswolds that is so beguiling... the beauty, the charming quirkiness of the locals, the architecture and the food (she makes the reader drool).
COTSWOLDS MEMOIR will hook you from the very first page. It's well researched with good information, but it is also filled with entertaining anecdotes. I was really sorry when I reached the end.

If you haven't visited the Cotswolds — or even if you have — you'll want to pack your bags and go!

— Monica B. Morris
Goodnight Children Everywhere **(The History Press)**

It's enchanting... very funny... Diz White has written a book that is part memoir, part travelogue and part stand-up comedy, summoning trips back and forth between Los Angeles and a bucolic sliver of England... She paints a nostalgic and affectionate canvas.

— **Steven Leigh Morris**
Critic-at-Large, LA Weekly

This book is captivating and enchanting... the writing is fluid, warm, and friendly. Diz draws the reader into her heart from the moment the book opens. She uses all the senses, like taste, scents and sight to get the reader involved in the drama. There are many physical images of her excursions and her quest.

Although it doesn't seem like buying a cottage would make for an exciting story, Diz has made it into a delightful and fun-filled adventure.

It will be easy for the reader to relate to her problems and sympathize. Wisdom about life and human foibles filter through the anecdotes and struggles.

— **William Greenleaf**
William Greenleaf Literary

Diz White vividly brings to life these charming Costwolds characters. Very funny stuff.

Mary Lou Belli
Directors Tell the Story: Master the Craft of Television and Film Directing **(Focal Press)**

Cotswolds Memoir

Discovering a Beautiful Region of Britain
On a Quest to Buy a 17th Century Cottage

by

Diz White

Cotswolds Memoir
Discovering a Beautiful Region of Britain
On a Quest to Buy a 17th Century Cottage

by

Diz White

ISBN: 978-0-9571162-0-7

Published by Larrabee Libraries, a Division of Larrabee Industries, in conjunction with Writersworld. This book is produced entirely in the UK, is available to order from most book shops in the United Kingdom, and is globally available via UK-based Internet book retailers and www.amazon.com.

Copy edited by Ian Large

Cover design by Randall Montgomery and Jag Lall

www.writersworld.co.uk

WRITERSWORLD
2 Bear Close Flats
Bear Close
Woodstock
Oxfordshire
OX20 1JX
England

The text pages of this book are produced via an independent certification process that ensures the trees from which the paper is produced come from well-managed sources that exclude the risk of using illegally logged timber while leaving options to use post-consumer recycled paper as well.

Contents

About the Author

British born Diz White divides her time between her beloved Cotswolds and Hollywood where she pursues a career as an actress, comedy writer and producer for films and television. Her acting work ranges from *Star Trek: Next Generation* to *Bullshot* the comedy movie, now a cult hit, in which she starred for HandMade Films. Diz received a New York Critics *Drama Desk Award* for her role in *El Grande de Coca-Cola* and this show, which she co-wrote, was subsequently filmed as a comedy special for HBO.

Also, Diz is the author of *Haunted Cotswolds* and *Haunted Cheltenham,* both published by The History Press. In addition to writing *The Comedy Group Book* (Smith and Kraus) Diz authored three plays for Samuel French Playscripts: *El Grande de Coca-Cola, Bullshot Crummond* and *Footlight Frenzy.*

Diz's favourite occupation is writing about her passion – the Cotswolds – as this gives her the opportunity of exploring this halcyon region and learning more of its history and culture. Together with her husband Randall Montgomery, Diz recently toured the Cotswolds shooting stunning footage for a DVD she produced with him entitled *GHOSTS OF GREAT BRITAIN COLLECTION – Haunted Cotswolds* (available on Amazon).

Diz is currently hard at work on a screenplay entitled *Stunt School,* a new theatre play and a teleplay of *COTSWOLDS MEMOIR – Discovering a Beautiful Region of Britain On a Quest to Buy a 17th Century Cottage.*

Diz can be reached through her website www.dizwhite.com and through www.writersworld.co.uk/cotswolds_memoirs.html

Other Books by this Author

Haunted Cotswolds (The History Press)
Haunted Cheltenham (The History Press)
The Comedy Group Book (Smith and Kraus)
El Grande de Coca-Cola (Samuel French Play scripts)
Bullshot Crummond (Samuel French Play scripts)
Footlight Frenzy (Samuel French Play scripts)

Other Media by this Author

DVD – *GHOSTS OF GREAT BRITAIN COLLECTION* –
Haunted Cotswolds (Available on Amazon)

MOVIE – now in DVD — *BULLSHOT* (HandMade
Films) (Available on Amazon)

A portion of the proceeds of this book will be donated to conservation institutions that benefit the Cotswolds region. This region is a designated AONB (Area of Outstanding Natural Beauty), and is overseen by the Cotswolds Conservation Board.

Acknowledgements

I thank with all my heart the people who have made this book possible.

They include: Graham Cook for his expertise, support and terrific team. Monica B. Morris, author of *Goodnight Children Everywhere* (The History Press) and numerous other books, for her counsel and for informing me that my 'author voice' comes through loud and clear; Joe Pistachio, who laughed so loudly while reading the manuscript of my book in bed late at night, that he narrowly missed having divorce papers served on him by his sleep-deprived wife Lisa, and Linda Cook who gave enthusiastic encouragement and lots of love. My lovely sister Linda who inspired this book; Wanda Ventham and Tim Carlton, fellow Cotswolds aficionados – their friendship means so much; Coral Oswald and her family. Also, Vivian Matalon, Gil Tobon, Sally Landsberg, Jason Lavitt, Joe Perrotti, Mariette Vandermolen and Dr. Claire Bland.

And most of all... I thank my dear husband and clever, patient helpmate Randall Montgomery, who makes me feel like tap dancing all day long. His photographic, graphic, editing and computer expertise do so much to enhance this book. In addition, his loving encouragement and willingness to put up with me through all the stages of getting this book to print were above and beyond anything that can be imagined.

Finally, I thank all the inhabitants of the Cotswolds, surely the most beautiful place on Earth, who gave me their stories, hospitality and warmth during the wonderful adventure of writing this book.

An Introduction

Come with me, on my journey. Tag along as I follow my bliss on a quest to buy a seventeenth century cottage in one of the most beautiful places in the world – the Cotswolds region of the English countryside.

I am English born, married to an American, and have lived in the United States for a number of years while pursuing a career in film and television acting and screenplay writing. Recently, however, my roots began to pull me back, giving focus to my long-held dream of owning a cottage in England.

My husband joined me in my search which encompasses all my passions – I'm a foodie, a history buff, a nature lover and I love to laugh – I am a comedienne after all. I'm also a terrific lookey-loo (I can't get enough of viewing old houses and fantasizing about how I would remodel them). I collect people as well; the more quirkily amusing and eccentric the better.

My roller-coaster, laughter-filled ride in search of my dream cottage is packed with many highs, heartbreaks and cliff-hangers *en route* but with so much of interest too.

Along the way I was charged by an angry bull called Chasin' Mason, I explored Roman settlements, fifteenth century villages, Domesday churches, archaeology digs, and open gardens. I enjoyed pub walks, won a welly wanging contest and hiked to the top of Haresfield Beacon. I supped on Seafood Panache, hog roasts, Broadfield farm beef, Southrop lamb and sampled every 'good life' delight the Cotswolds has to offer.

The love I developed for this region and its colourful inhabitants engendered a feeling of community missing from my busy urban existence. When many obstacles barred my way the serenity I felt each time I arrived in the Cotswolds sustained my resolve, and gave incentive to my Herculean efforts to raise enough money to finance my dream cottage.

There were many hilarious adventures as I took every crazy job that came my way, zipping back and forth between my frenetic Hollywood career and the peace and beauty of the English countryside.

The wonderful fact is that almost every inch of the Cotswolds is exquisite from its meandering single track lanes that lead into untouched-by-time medieval villages to breathtaking vistas of undulating hills, resplendent in their patchwork of multi-coloured crops, divided by honey-hued dry stone walls that wend their way in gentle curves across sheep-dotted hills.

It is unfortunate, therefore, to see visitors being directed to the same few villages, perfect as they are, when there is so much more to enjoy. Many of my off-the-beaten-track Cotswolds explorations are overlooked in tourist information and I am very happy to pass on the results of my sojourns to interested readers. I have found that there is nothing to compare with getting away from the madding crowd and hiking along the windswept banks of the River Windrush, or the trails of the Cotswold Way, with their spectacular views, or taking a pub walk to a remote village and exploring the misty waters of the upper reaches of the Thames.

My passion for the Cotswolds also extends to its conservation and if the reader shares my interest there is information concerning this in the visitor guide at the end of my narrative.

This book is my love note to the halcyon Cotswolds and its people, a souvenir of time spent in this enchanting region.

Should you decide to come along, you can join me for afternoon tea on the lawn of my hard won prize, followed by a lazy, sunny boat ride on the nearby River Thames as my husband strums his ukulele and croons to the lilt of *Life is Just a Bowl of Cherries*. It doesn't get much better than this.

Diz White, January 2012

Kelmscott Manor, home of William Morris

**Photography
by
Randall Montgomery**

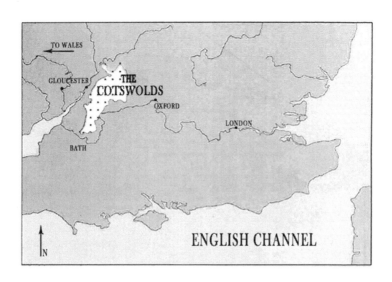

The Cotswolds

Near Temple Guiting

For my husband Randall with love
My mother Josephine Ashley, the poet
and my dear family

One

FOLLOWING MY BLISS TO THE COTSWOLDS
Shilton, Great Tew, Bath

'Come on you two, get off your big fat bums and help me catch the donkey! He's halfway to Dickleburgh by now!' The local postmistress dragged my mother and me out of our comfortable garden chairs before she tore off, yelling for more volunteers. We felt strangely compelled to do as she said and soon found ourselves following her down the leafy lane of a small village in the English countryside.

It was my mother who got me interested in spending time in the country. She was quite a character, my mother. When my old sod of a father died, I encouraged her to marry again, and to get her thinking along those lines, I asked her to name someone she fancied. I told her to pick any man in the world, someone like the actor Patrick Stewart perhaps. She thought for a few seconds and then said, 'Josef Stalin.'

'Stalin,' I protested, 'but Mum, he sent thousands of people to Siberia and they never came back. How could you possibly fancy him?'

She replied, 'Well, he's no worse than your father, dear.'

She decided not to pursue any more relationships for the moment and instead filled her time with gentle trips to small villages, where she pottered around antique fairs and rummage sales. As a poor East End kid, she had made drawings of chickens with four legs, because she had never seen one on a farm. Her first visit to the country as a young woman had been such a revelation that she would be transported when she talked about it. Her descriptions were so poetic that I began to share in her enthusiasm, and the next summer, when she rented a cottage in the country for a week, I tagged along. After

1

escaping the screaming boredom of the London suburbs, I found myself as fascinated as my mother had been on her first visit to a small village. It was like a trip to a foreign land or even another universe. The perfume of roasted saddle of lamb with apricots and garlic, the fragrance of a raft of June roses, the feel of the uneven flagstones of a 1,000-year-old church, the taste of a handful of ripe blackberries greedily snatched from a centuries-old hedgerow, made me giddy with joy.

I was charmed, too, by the local people. They had colour, life, eccentricities, funny speech, wooden legs and buck teeth. Each one of them also had something I dimly recognised after living too long in the suburbs – a soul.

The race was on. We followed the postmistress as she gave chase to a donkey that could just be seen making dust on its way to Dickleburgh. It had escaped from its paddock and everybody in the village yelled, panted and stumped after it. We tried to keep up with the crowd – the young, the old, the local hairdresser (scissors still in hand) a pack of yapping dogs and a mad granddad in a wheelchair yelling, 'Grab the bastard's tail!' This he actually managed to do, when the donkey, cheekily taunting his followers, trotted a little too close. For a few glorious seconds the old granddad was pulled along, at a high rate of speed, bumping and screaming until his wheelchair skidded over and he tumbled out.

As we reached the next village, yells of triumph from all the villagers deafened us as they almost caught the donkey. But suddenly he broke free, wheeled around and cantered back to our village. When we returned, he was happily munching hay in his paddock with a sly look in his eye.

Apparently, chasing the donkey to Dickleburgh was a regular, cathartic ritual that all the villagers thoroughly enjoyed. Nothing like this happened in the suburbs – I was hooked.

The next opportunity we had to get to the country was when I was in college and my mother invited me to join her for a holiday – a few days at a bed and breakfast on a working farm near Shilton in the Cotswolds. As we drove to our destination, I became enchanted by this region. I couldn't believe how lovely it was. The quiet country lanes would lead out to spectacular views of gently rolling hills covered in a patchwork of fields. Unspoilt countryside stretched as far as the eye could see, with an occasional church spire to guide the way to yet another ancient village. The Cotswolds are located just east and a little bit south of Wales and north of the city of Bath. For several centuries its inhabitants made oodles of money from wool manufacture. When this trade failed, the poverty it created prevented the rapid growth and building booms that made other parts of Great Britain look like winners in the 'Ugliest New Building in the World' contest.

Visitors to the Cotswolds are usually directed to the chocolate-box, picture-perfect villages. I was thankful that our route took us along narrow lanes, far away from these areas and showed a wilder, more interesting Cotswolds. I had a feeling of stepping back in time as I passed through these small hamlets in their lush green settings. The local Cotswold stone is a honey colour that causes buildings to glow in the sunset; this, together with the dry stone walls and the ancient hedgerows, create a beautiful landscape that is largely unchanged since the sixteenth century.

Shilton is cosily tucked away in the Shill Brook Valley and is close to Burford. At its centre is a forded road leading to a farm with a dovecot. Cars crossing the ford must travel slowly to avoid the ducks swimming by. A stream runs through Shilton's rose-bedecked gardens, the village pond is lined with chestnut trees and the Norman church to the south of the village features fourteenth century carvings showing scenes from the Passion.

We found our digs, were greeted by the farmer's wife and shown to our room overlooking the cow shed. After settling in, we ordered a taxi to take us to dinner in a nearby village that evening in order to meet some friends. We promised ourselves, however, that we would soon visit Shilton's pub, The Rose and Crown, with its reputation for excellent food and charming terraced garden, as soon as we could.

'I can take you at eight o'clock but no sooner 'cos I've got to milk the cows first.' We were amused to find that our taxi driver was also a cowman on the farm where we were staying. Fortunately, he managed to change out of his muddy Wellington boots before picking us up.

Safely delivered to the bar of the pub in the next village, we were enjoying our pre-dinner sherry when our ears were assaulted by a piano player loudly murdering show tunes in the dining area nearby. Dressed in a fancy smoking jacket, with a candelabra perched on top of a piano strewn with sheet music, he must have thought he was Liberace as he thumped away using extravagant hand gestures. He was so intent on charming his audience that he failed to notice that the vibrations from his vigorous playing had caused a lighted candle to fall onto his music. Interpreting warning cries from the diners as shouts of approval for his playing, he showed off with a few more rippling *glissandos* as the sheet music on top of his piano burst into flames. Screaming waitresses doused the fire with jugs of water, while Liberace flapped his arms in hysteria and ran around in circles. It was great cabaret.

The timeless beauty of the area and the unselfconscious dottiness of some of its inhabitants put a spell on me and I formed the ambition, there and then, that I would one day live in one of these villages and buy my own Cotswold cottage.

Although I had planned to accompany my mother on more trips like this, a career in theatre and the movies whirled me away to distant parts. But I never forgot my visit to this lovely place.

Some years later I was finally in a position to try and make my dream come true. I was now living in California with my American husband, Randall. Known as Randy, he was aware of the double-entendre nature of his name in England – nevertheless, he was an Anglophile who longed for a cottage in the Cotswolds as much as I did. Although I liked my American home, I began noticing some homesickness for the English countryside – my roots were pulling me back. One of the symptoms of my condition seemed to be a craving for heaps of Yorkshire puddings. When I couldn't find them cooked properly in restaurants, I was forced to make them myself in order to feed my habit. This only made things worse, so next I tried to squelch my longing for my homeland by watching zillions of English movies. The only thing this did for me was make me realise that Michael Caine is in every English film that has ever been made. There was nothing for it but the real thing – it was time for action.

The quest to find our own Cotswold cottage had begun. The first part of the plan involved a reality check. Would we really like it? We mulled this over. What would it be like to spend extended time in a cottage in the country? My husband was keen on the idea but wasn't sure he wanted to move to England permanently, but maybe for part of the year? I wondered how that would work. Was my desire to do this idealised fantasy? Perhaps the reality wouldn't match up. Even if it did, would my husband find spending more time in England too alien after a life spent in the US? These questions would need answers before we could commit to buying property.

I had high hopes, however, as Randy and I had already had a taste of visiting the English countryside together when we had chosen it for the location of our wedding. At the time, my mother was living in the village of Snettisham in Norfolk. I loved this place, although I found I had to wait until a sneeze was coming on if I wanted to pronounce its name like a local – 'Schnes(tishoo)haaammm'. Randy and I loved it so much, in fact, that we started planning for the nuptials right away.

On the day of our wedding, a horse and trap took us to the church. It was a beautiful ride through the country lanes on a sunny day. All that could be heard was the clip clop of the horse's hooves and the singing of the birds. Everything seemed picture-book perfect when the old boy who was driving the trap turned around and fixed his gaze upon us. Expecting him to point out a local landmark or to comment on the splendour of our wedding party, we were startled to hear him say, 'You'll have to get out of the trap, Billy, my horse, can't pull you over the hill – YOU'RE TOO FAT!' As I had slimmed down to a size ten for my wedding day, this was not the kind of thing I wanted to hear.

We got out and Billy pulled the trap slowly over the small incline. On the way back after the church ceremony, the horse was suddenly full of pep, trotting along quite briskly. When I inquired about this the old boy replied, 'Well, when you was in the church I gave Billy a pint of Guinness.'

Back in Los Angeles, we talked often about the English countryside. Randy had enjoyed it all so much that he was quite amenable to our dipping our toes in the water by going for a visit to the Cotswolds. We agreed that we should get a feeling for what it was like to live in England again before we started any kind of cottage shopping.

We saved all our spare money for the longest vacation we could manage – three weeks – and, the following summer, rented an old cottage in a village a good distance from the tourist part of the Cotswolds.

On the plane to Heathrow, I realised that my husband would need a refresher course in British catchphrases as they can seem like a foreign language to Americans. I reminded him that many of them have a subtext and can't always be taken at face value.

We encountered the first phrase of this nature in the car hire office when we heard the agent say '*bear with me*'. In this instance this could mean anything from, 'You stand there staring into space for ten minutes while I push buttons on my keyboard with no result,' to, 'As I have carelessly erased you from the system, I am going to have to stall for half an hour and still not provide you with the car you want.'

The phrase *at the end of the day* signals the beginning of a philosophical discussion of how the car hire company can justify substituting a three-wheel Czech-made Skoda for the Vauxhall Vectra that had been ordered.

When you ask for some extras, you are told that it is *more than my job's worth* which means, 'Granting your wish would be immensely helpful to you but slightly inconvenient to me, so therefore you are on your own.'

During the wait for the car, I translated several more key phrases for my husband that I knew we would encounter during our stay:

Mustn't grumble: My house has been struck by lightning, my husband's leaving me for another man and my children just got arrested, but I enjoy being a martyr so I won't complain.

I've only got two hands: I am lazy and uncooperative so, not only will I refuse to honour your request, I'll make you feel guilty for making it to begin with.

I then warned Randy that we British love clichés and sometimes will make up entire sentences of them. This was immediately demonstrated by the car hire agent as he handed us the keys to the Skoda.

'Look on the bright side, Sir, re your car i.e. at the end of the day, your car – vis-à-vis a Vauxhall – has been replaced with a Skoda, when all is said and done, sir, needs drive as the devil must after all *honi soit qui mal y pense* – excuse my French – nothing to lose your nut over. Mind how you go.'

It took about an hour and a half to drive our Skoda from Heathrow to the Cotswolds. We had found our rental cottage through an agency in Boston. At first we were interested in a cottage that the agency suggested in Great Tew.

This charming village in Oxfordshire is situated about five miles north east of Chipping Norton and almost all its cottages are thatched. The pictures we were sent also showed the quaint Falkland Arms public house, which was built in the sixteenth century and originally named The Horse and Groom. Its cosy interior, sporting huge oak beams, resembles an ancient galleon with primitive wood furniture and a low ceiling festooned with dozens of china mugs. Clay pipes and snuff can be purchased at the bar and the publican offers an impressive range of different beers. The original old stone spiral staircase leads upstairs to recently remodelled bedrooms with four-poster beds and antique furniture. This pub is named after Lucius Cary the 2nd Viscount Falkland. In 1630 the Viscount gathered together a group of writers, scholars, philosophers and theologians at Great Tew and these included Ben Jonson and Abraham Cowley.

As beautiful as this almost perfectly preserved village appeared to be we decided we preferred a more remote part of the Cotswolds that featured the classic slate roofs and Cotswold stone walls. Our final choice, Stable Cottage, belonged to a retired army officer and his wife who let it to holidaymakers. It was in a small village in the southern part of the Cotswolds.

We had rented it sight unseen, as no pictures had been available, but we were urged to take it immediately as it would be snapped up long before the pictures came in. We came across a big manor house first, tucked away down a quiet leafy lane. It was one of those wonderful old piles that looked as if a new wing had been added about every century. Nobody was around, so we wandered through a number of outbuildings and into the grounds that surrounded the property. They were vast and luxuriously planted with massive trees and flowering shrubs. We crossed a seemingly endless lawn and finally found our cottage in another stand of trees and shrubs. It had its own garden circled by a centuries-old dry stone wall. This garden within a garden was magical. There was a feeling of limitless outdoor rooms created by clearings between the trees and shrubs. And, beyond that, the grounds blended into the fields of the surrounding farms.

The cottage was seventeenth century, with foot-thick walls and sagging, uneven roof tiles so covered in moss and lichens that they had acquired an uneven patina and a dozen different hues. I could almost feel the ghosts of the groomsmen who had inhabited it in centuries past. It was completely quiet except for the whisper of the leaves rustling in the tall trees that towered overhead.

Brigadier and the Hon. Mrs Murgatroyd owned Stable Cottage, the rambling manor house and the entire village that surrounded them, as their family had done for the past three or four hundred years. The Brigadier came from a long line of aristocratic army officers and his wife had the title of 'honourable' so she must have been the younger daughter of a baron or a viscount.

Our first impression was that their village had been preserved in aspic, as though it had been forgotten by time. The Brigadier and Mrs Murgatroyd's only concession to the present day was to rent out several of the cottages and houses they owned in their grounds and others in their village. They, like many members of the aristocracy in Britain today, were finding ways to pay for the upkeep of their large manor houses. Despite this, the Brigadier firmly knew his place, in a very feudal way, as the village squire, and expected its inhabitants, who all worked for him, to know their place too.

Mrs Murgatroyd came down from the manor house to greet us. I found her fascinating as this was one of my first encounters with the English aristocracy. Everything about her was different, from her clothes, which were exquisite, to her manners and speech. To me, she embodied everything that money, breeding and an upper class society could produce. My own upbringing had been somewhat different. I came from the East End of London, and my family moved out to a town called Rainham, in Essex, which was in the process of being swallowed up by the London suburban sprawl. I was a teenager when we arrived and there wasn't an English aristocrat in sight. I remember being amazed at the motley crowd that made up the inhabitants of this town. The inbreeding of several centuries and an isolated location had contributed to an eye-popping assortment of mutants. These, no doubt, were a result of the limited gene pool opportunities. I was amazed that our milkman had two thumbs on his left hand and his daughter, who sat next to me in school, had two thumbs on her right hand. A woman who lived in the next street had a protrusion growing out of her shin that looked like a third leg; the local village idiot known, politically incorrectly, as the 'niff noff', had no roof to his mouth; and the road sweeper was convinced he was Prince Phillip. These bizarre characters were all getting mixed up with the Cockney invasion on its march to suburbia.

Coming from this background, therefore, I was a little in awe of the fact that we would be renting from upper class English army types, especially since they seemed to be living as if nothing had changed in the last hundred years. After we had settled in, Mrs Murgatroyd invited us up to the manor house for drinks.

We arrived at the cocktail hour and were shown into our hosts' drawing room by a butler in a fraying tail coat. He took an enormously long time to take our coats, hang them up and shuffle down a long hallway before he arrived at the drawing room and announced us. The Brigadier, who was extremely tall and very ancient, seemed to unfold as he rose from a low chintz sofa. For most of the time he had a stern expression but every so often his eyes betrayed a cheeky twinkle that he tried to hide. Mrs M. was pleasantly plump, with a shock of carefully hennaed red hair. She had a tremendous dignity and elegance about her and a very charming manner. I found, however, that our communication with both her and the Brigadier were complicated by several things. To begin with, Mrs Murgatroyd's class background was so different from mine that we spoke, in essence, a different language. This, combined with the deafness and innate dottiness of these two old dears, meant that there were some hilarious misunderstandings.

When Mrs Murgatroyd first greeted us she said, 'You must be tired after your flight. Do you have everything you need?' Randy replied with jet-lagged brevity, 'Bath would be nice.'

'Really, sight-seeing already?' Mrs Murgatroyd said. 'The first thing I would want is a bath.'

'But that is the first thing I want.'

'Then why are you talking about gallivanting off to Bath?' Mrs Murgatroyd was referring to the nearby town of Bath.

My husband replied, 'I wasn't, but that would be nice too.'

Detail above door lintel, Bath

Mrs Murgatroyd cottoned on to her mistake. 'Oh, how silly of me! When you said bath, I thought you meant Bath not bath. Did you want to take a bath or go to Bath or both? If you go to Bath you'll find it's a lovely town, south of the M4 motorway. It has a two thousand year old Roman bath, in perfect repair, that is heated by natural hot springs and you will find the Assembly Rooms which have been there since the seventeenth century, I think, are wonderful for afternoon tea. There's usually a string quartet playing, very elegantly, and they give you glasses of the spa water to drink as well. It tastes absolutely ghastly, smells of bad eggs you see, but it does

pep you up. The antique shops are quite marvellous and
so is the architecture. It's all Georgian – and there is one
beautiful white stone crescent of houses after another.
Quite breathtaking, really, when it is viewed from the top
of the hill. You must go and visit, oh... but look at the
time. It'll all be closed if you go now.'

'Forget it. How 'bout a shower?'

Mrs Murgatroyd completely unfazed by this exchange,
continued, 'Oh that reminds me. There's a new water
heater in your cottage. You'll have to turn it on to heat
the bath water. It's very important that it's done right or
it could explode. I've asked Pilkins our handyman to
come and explain. I want you to meet him anyway
because he will also be popping in unexpectedly now and
then to mow your lawn.'

Randy replied jokingly, 'Oh really? Then we'd better
make sure we keep our clothes on when we're
sunbathing.'

Mrs Murgatroyd, not getting the joke, looked very
alarmed, 'You're not like the Fortesques are you?'

'The Fortesques?'

'They rented Stable Cottage last June. You're not
nudists like they are, are you?' asked Mrs Murgatroyd.

'Don't worry. There's more chance of us jumping off
the church steeple.'

Mrs Murgatroyd, again not getting the joke, now went
into panic mode, 'Good Heavens! You're not Bungee
Plungers too? The church steeple won't take your weight.
It needs repair.'

In order to calm Mrs Murgatroyd down, Randy found
himself saying a sentence that might have come out of a
grown-up version of Alice in Wonderland.

'We promise not to bungee plunge nude off the church
steeple.'

'Thank you, how kind!' Now Mrs Murgatroyd suddenly
showed genuine concern, 'It won't spoil your holiday will
it?'

Before we could reply, Pilkins the handyman
appeared at the door pulling on his forelock and
muttering under his breath.

'Pilkins,' said Mrs Murgatroyd, 'tell the Americans how to switch on the new boiler so that it won't explode. Pay attention,' she whispered to us, 'Pilkins is very impatient and he'll only tell anybody anything once.'

Pilkins's reply, combining an unintelligible country accent, a speech impediment and ill-fitting false teeth, produced an amazing jumble of sounds. These were accompanied by an assortment of violent body spasms.

'[Whistle] Ye dee like thisss [whistle, click] see, step one. Wend up the flanges, [raspberry] cocking rheostat [arms pumping] before you wangle the jib lever. Step toeey, [whistle, pop, slurp] pull the grimble bladder and step free, sprackle the back rings [kicking motion] until the tibble bumps clock on the doodle jims, scheeee? [hiccup]'

We stared, open mouthed, at this performance before realising that we had been too fascinated to make sense of one word of it. Mrs Murgatroyd, smiling broadly, said, 'There you are, clear as a bell.'

Two

ROMAN RUINS AND A QUEST FOR A COTTAGE
Sapperton, Quenington, Chedworth

The next morning, thankfully unblownup by the water heater, we sat on the terrace of our cottage looking at a *What's On* guide, together with several books of local pub walks written by a man with the interesting name of Nigel Vile. We picked out hikes to take in areas we had never previously explored, as well as those found in places we thought we might want to settle should we decide to buy a cottage.

We wanted to avoid villages like Upper and Lower Slaughter, Bourton-on-the-Water and Shipton-under-Wychwood, with their thousands of visitors, in favour of areas that were not so camera-ready.

With this idea in mind, we leafed through our pub walks book looking for hikes that were well off the beaten track. Randy's choices were often influenced, however, by whether a pub stocked his favourite beer. We were anxious to shake off our jet lag and thought that a healthy hike, followed by a boozy pub lunch, would be just the ticket. Of course, I knew it wouldn't be long before we were bagging the hike and just doing the boozy lunch but, at least, we were starting out with good intentions.

I left Randy to plan our walk as I basked in the peace and sunshine of the garden. Cooing woodpigeons were the only sounds to be heard as I strolled around. I noticed tiny, wild strawberries growing through the cracks in the flagstones, a well-stocked herbaceous border and dozens of peach-coloured roses. A little later I made some tea and toast and was ready to enjoy one of my favourite pastimes – reading an English newspaper.

I had forgotten how much they amused me. The World over, there are people who are born without a brain, but to my joy British newspapers turn their mishaps into delightfully entertaining stories.

Today's prize went to officials of the Post Office, who obviously valued political correctness over practicality. One of their workers had been caught unceremoniously disposing of his deliveries. It turns out that when he was being interviewed for the job he had truthfully told the postal authorities that he was dyslexic. The Post Office types told him they didn't discriminate against people with disabilities, so he got the job. However, when he couldn't read the addresses on the letters and discarded them in a field, they arrested him. That's mighty bighearted of them, I thought. What's next, I mused, tone-deaf piano tuners? Pilots who are afraid of heights? Or maybe anorexic chefs?

Our first pub walk from Nigel Vile's book took us to the isolated Frome Valley, between Cirencester and Stroud, near the village of Sapperton. This walk runs alongside the Sapperton Tunnel, a deserted canal waterway that was built in the late eighteenth century by miners from various parts of the country.

There was once an extensive canal system in England and, before the invention of the steam engine, the boats that carried goods along it were drawn by horses along the canal paths. I discovered an interesting book, *The Flower of Gloster* that describes the author Ernest Temple Thurston's journey by canal along the entire length of the Thames and Severn Canal, of which the Sapperton Tunnel was part, just before it was closed to through traffic in 1911.

His description of the Cotswolds part of the canal from over a century ago with its colourful characters and a visit to the Red Lion Pub in Cropredy (still existing today) paints a charming picture of this long-ago era and its gentle pace of life.

Various volunteer bodies have helped restore a large section of the Thames and Severn Canal and their goal is to one day make a navigable link between the Upper

Thames and Oxford so that the stunning scenery of this region can be viewed entirely from the water.

The Daneway Inn, which had housed the workers who built the Sapperton Tunnel, sits above the overgrown path at the beginning of the walk. Randy and I had lunch there and as we wandered around awaiting our order, noticed that it was made up of three cottages joined together. We were served a steak sandwich that covered a large dinner plate, along with a pint of very good beer.

It was a hot, sultry day but it didn't bother us as our walk was shaded by trees meeting overhead. We were delighted to see that the hike included Siccaridge Wood Nature Reserve which was full of traditional flora, some of it quite rare. We hiked for an hour or so along the disused canal and were thoroughly enjoying ourselves. Towards the end of the hour, however, clouds gathered overhead and thunderclaps could be heard close by.

Just as it started bucketing down, we got lost. We thought that Nigel, the author of our pub walks book, was very Vile indeed since his directions didn't seem to make sense. We had to cross an open field, we thought, to get back to Sapperton, but before we had reached the other side we were drenched with rain and several inches taller due to the mud that had collected on the soles of our hiking boots. We were instantly so wet that we just stood still and laughed as rivulets of water streamed down our necks and soaked us to the skin.

We found out later that everybody gets lost at this exact point of the hike (to be fair to old Nigel Vile, he does put a disclaimer in the front of his book saying that routes and landmarks do change).

It was scary but exhilarating to be completely lost, with thunder booming overhead and rain lashing down so hard that it seemed to bounce back up from the ground to waist level. When we finally found our way back, we looked as if we had been mud wrestling for three days. After this, I thought my husband would be ready to go back to America on the next plane out, but he thought it had been a terrific adventure and said that getting lost was the most fun of all. Randy wanted to get our bearings and finish the last part of the walk, but I was too muddy. Our pub walks book described the remainder of the route which featured a wonderful view of the Frome Valley and, further on, St Kenelm's Church, which contains some terrific woodwork from an old manor house. It would, however, have to wait for another hike.

The next day, Saturday, was hot and sunny, and seemed perfect for a visit to a village fête in nearby Quenington. This village is two miles north of Fairford on the slopes of the River Coln. Quenington is noted for one of its nineteenth century homes, which features a thirteenth century gatehouse and a dovecot of the same period. The church suffers from a Victorian remodel but left intact are the Norman north and south doorways and each has a beautifully carved tympanum. The south doorway depicts The Coronation of the Virgin and the north The Harrowing of Hell. Both are exceptional examples of Romanesque art.

This was to be Randy's first fête and I explained that these events are usually held to raise money for the church roof fund or for some other community activity and are great excuses for all the villagers to gather together to get drunk, overeat, insult the vicar and injure themselves or their children in any number of arcane contests like Welly Wanging, Greasy Pole Fighting or Splat the Rat.

We parked on the outskirts of the village and on our way to the fête struck up a conversation with a couple who were sitting in their front garden. We were interested in their cottage as an estate agent's board outside announced that it was for sale. They saw us looking at their home and offered to show it to us right then without bothering to make a formal appointment.

As they were doing so, the husband, Jim, chatted on about its history. His wife Eileen had grown up in the cottage. She had later travelled abroad where they met and married. Jim and Eileen came back to England where he was to meet her parents for the first time. The parents were then living in this same cottage and Jim and Eileen arrived so late in the evening that all of

Eileen's family had retired to bed. There was a heat wave at the time, and Jim and Eileen slept *au naturel*.

The next morning, Eileen's mother, eager to meet her new son-in-law, brought in an early morning tray of tea. As she opened the door, the family's giant dog pushed in front of her and bounded onto the bed with such force that Jim was propelled out of it and crashed to the floor. This was his mother-in-law's first sight of him – screaming with fear, and totally naked!

We liked the Cotswolds more and more. This area seemed to be filled with interesting characters whose manner was so friendly that they were willing to tell us embarrassing stories about their first meeting with their mother-in-law barely thirty seconds after being introduced.

Afterwards, we agreed that the house we had just seen wouldn't be suitable for us, but it was great to have viewed our first cottage. We hadn't even made a decision about buying in the Cotswolds and here we were looky-looing already.

By the time we reached the village green, the fête was in full swing. The entire area was crowded with families playing games, or hanging out at bric-a-brac stalls, raffle booths, barbecues, tea tents and various contests. Villagers strolled around happily in the sun and hordes of kids were streaking around yelling and laughing.

A whole hog was being roasted on a spit and as my husband needs feeding every hour on the hour we made straight for it. We were served a massive sandwich and chowed down on big chunks of pork. The crackling that accompanied it was so brittle that it snapped with the sound of rifle shots. Piled on top of everything was a big wodge of sage stuffing and goops of apple sauce. This sandwich, washed down with a couple of glasses of beer, was as delicious as any *haute cuisine* dish I had ever had.

As we ate, we sat and watched the children from the local school put on a dance exhibition. They were so young, sweet and innocent it made me want to cry.

Towards the end of the exhibition a boot whizzed past our heads. A cry of 'Control your welly!' made us realise that the welly wanging contest was going on behind us. This contest consists of throwing a rubber boot at a target a few yards away. There is a prize for hitting the bullseye. If you have ever tried to throw a Wellington boot (and why would you have?) you realise that it is impossible to achieve any kind of accuracy. No matter where you aim it, the boot flies off in a totally unpredictable direction. As a result, during the fête, there is the danger of the odd boot occasionally raining down on the crowd, braining someone, squishing ice creams or landing on a roasting hog.

Afterwards, we ambled over to where the members of a smartly uniformed brass band were sitting around on a break, and Randy, ever ready to relive his glory days as a trumpet player in his high school marching band, couldn't resist chatting to their leader. When the musicians reassembled a few minutes later, it was obvious that the band leader had taken note of my husband's American accent and the fact that the date actually was the 4th of July, because the band struck up a wonderfully wonky, oompah-oompah version of the *Star Spangled Banner.* Randy dutifully stood with his hand on his heart.

The music made a jaunty accompaniment to all the frenetic activity of the fête and, as we moved on, we were amused by the different games and contests. Among them were: Nine Pins, a Monster Vegetable contest, Tug of War, Duck Races, Aunt Sally, Beat the Goalie, Best Bitch Dog Show and many more. We laughed at the raffle prizes which were often incredibly impoverished, two of them being a cotton tea towel and a bottle of nail varnish.

The entire proceedings were punctuated, from time to time, by a stuttering, amateur MC on a public address system that crackled with static. We strained unsuccessfully to understand the announcement for the next event and it wasn't until I heard the unmistakable sound of jingling bells that I knew we were in for a Morris dance. Although it is performed differently, this could be called the English equivalent of Irish dancing and villagers have been performing it for hundreds of years.

These guys put on a great show even though it's a ridiculous thing for grown men to do. They were wearing funny-looking uniforms with shorts, long socks and bells tied around their legs. They danced, with much jumping up and down and slapping of their knees and ankles, like demented boy scouts who had just been stung by a swarm of bees.

By the end of the fête, I felt like a happy nine year old as I clutched balloons, hand-knitted dolls I had picked up at the bric-a-brac stall, a coconut and a stuffed animal won in a raffle. When we got back to our cottage, we went through our *What's On* and marked off every upcoming fête during our stay.

We chose the Chedworth Roman Villa for our next day's destination. I am crazy about archaeology and this site is one of the most important of all the Roman ruins in Britain. It is a half dozen miles north of Cirencester on the Stow-on-the-Wold road and very easy to reach.

Although the Romans invaded Britain in AD 43, the excavated mosaic floors of the baths in this villa looked as if they could have been laid down yesterday. There was room after room of mostly intact floors that still retained their bright colours and were imaginatively designed with swirling scenes of Neptune-type gods holding tridents and smiling.

Portions of the walls of the villa were still there, along with whole rooms including kitchens, a dining room and various outbuildings. It was fascinating to see how the Romans made an extensive network of cold, warm and hot plunges for these baths with names like *Tepidarium* and *Frigidarium*. We were clearly able to see how they had engineered the under-floor heating and plumbing for them. It was great that the site wasn't at all crowded and we were able to take our time seeing just how the Romans conducted their everyday life in England.

Excavation was still going on and we observed a crowd of young archaeology students painstakingly digging out more of the site. We started chatting to them and asking questions. They looked very serious and academic until Randy mentioned that I had worked on the film *Gladiator.* They immediately dropped their reserve.

'Wow, cool! Do you know Russell Crowe?'

I explained that I didn't because I had worked on the post-production sound after the film had been shot. Many of the women's voices yelling in the Coliseum were mine – my voice had been recorded and overlaid numerous times.

We then discovered the excellent shop where the historical books and other instructional aids far outnumbered the money-making souvenirs.

Next we took a walk leading on from the Roman villa by the River Coln and around Chedworth Woods. We worked up an appetite for our pub lunch, which we ate at the Seven Tuns pub in Chedworth Village a mile or so away. The cottages in this village are cosily tucked in among its hills and the Seven Tuns pub is below the church. We found out that the Tuns referred to in the pub's name were brewers' fermenting vats. The pub displayed many fascinating photos with some showing local characters lined up in cricket and football teams and others scenes from the Chedworth of years ago.

The day we were there, the publican served us a terrific lunch consisting of lamb with prunes, garlic, and red onion marmalade. This went well with the excellent draught beer. It couldn't have been a nicer day out: a lazy drive through the exquisite rolling hills, an old Roman ruin, a nifty walk and a tasty lunch. We finished off with a couple of coffees, sitting in the sunny pub garden, and even wedged in a nap. We spent most of the afternoon there before slowly heading back to our cottage through the country back lanes.

At the beginning of the trip, I had started a pros and cons list to try and make an objective decision about buying a home in the Cotswolds. So far, it was all pros and no cons. I tried to tell myself that we were on holiday and that, if we lived here, it could well be a different story. Somehow, though, I was having trouble convincing myself of this fact.

Randy was having a great time too. He loves music and plays several instruments, including the flute, the ukulele and the aforementioned trumpet. He also has a great singing voice and when he was courting me he used to leave love songs on my answering machine. Awww... he had figured out the best way to melt my stony cold heart.

He had gone in search of some live music and found jazz being played in the evenings at the Trout Pub on the Thames at Lechlade. The pub garden spills right down to the banks of the river, and the jazz bands that play there are very good. Throughout the summer a different group is featured every Sunday and Tuesday night.

We were surprised to see just how narrow the Thames was at this point and were told that its source was not far away (it turned out to be near the village of Coates which is five miles west of Cirencester). The next day we went in search of its starting point, envisioning perhaps a natural pool, but found instead that it was not even visible above ground. It seemed odd that the source of the mighty Thames was nowhere to be seen and merely marked by a granite plaque in the middle of a fallow field.

Back at the Trout Pub we discovered that it was possible to rent boats, and we began planning a trip down the Thames. We waited for a really hot day when the cool breeze of the river would be ideal, loaded up a packed picnic basket and Randy's ukulele, and hired a boat. We drifted slowly along the winding Thames. It is only forty or fifty yards wide at this point and threads its way through farms and stands of trees. Occasionally, Randy would row a little. Now and then a colourful narrow boat would pass us, its occupants giving a friendly wave. Sometimes we would drift by a clutch of ducks with their fluff-covered babies who would scoot nervously out of the way.

We had to pass through Buscot Lock to get to our destination of Kelmscott. The name Buscot seemed familiar, but I couldn't remember where I'd heard it until I recalled our first meeting with Brigadier Murgatroyd. Over drinks he had said to Randy, 'You should go to

Buscot. Its church has very high pews. It's a good church to go to if you don't want to be seen pinching your girlfriend's bottom.' As Mrs Murgatroyd glared at him he said, 'Watch out! Now I'm going to get a rocket.'

There are several locks along the upper reaches of the Thames, and it is quite an experience going through them. The lock keeper guides the boats into the lock, two or three at a time, and makes sure that everything is secured by closing the tall gates with a wheel. When a lock gate is opened at one end, it releases the water, which either raises or lowers the water level of the river. It's a surprise, the first time, to find the boat being lowered fifteen feet or so in just a minute and to see the slimy, green walls of the lock rising up on each side.

Arriving by river is the best way to see Kelmscott with its two dozen or so cottages clustered together by the Thames. We had a reservation to tour Kelmscott Manor, once the home of the famous Victorian designer and craftsman William Morris who, in 1871, along with the Pre-Raphaelite painter Dante Gabriel Rossetti, took a house there as his country retreat and studio. The manor is now owned by the Society of Antiquaries who restored and currently maintains it.

We tied up our boat and came upon the Plough Inn a few steps away. The pub looked as if it would be ideal for a meal and a drink on a summer evening with its cluster of tables in a flower-filled garden.

Next, we strolled through the ancient village, looking for Kelmscott Manor. I particularly wanted to visit this house because I had studied graphic design and illustration in London before I got into showbiz. The manor showcases Morris's designs. When we finally found it down a quiet lane on the edge of the village, it was so beautiful it made us gasp. We felt as if we had gone through a portal that had taken us back five centuries.

The manor is Tudor, built in 1570, with another wing added in 1670. Apparently William Morris chose it because it was completely unspoilt, and in harmony with the village and its surroundings. It still is, and you can practically taste its age – it is so delicious.

The gabled three-storey house was built in the traditional farmhouse style in Cotswolds stone. The wing that had been added a hundred years later shows the influence of the Renaissance with its classical pediments above the windows and the fine wood panelling inside its rooms.

Together with a small group of other visitors we were taken through the house by one of the volunteer guides. It looked as if Mr Morris had just stepped out for a pipe of tobacco as everything he owned was still in place. This included furniture, paintings and masses of his wonderful designs of wallpapers and chintzes that are known the world over. This was so clearly a house and not a museum that you could practically see the Morris family moving about in the background.

The Renaissance wing contained a sitting room with white Georgian panelling that managed to be both cosy and grand. The room above had tapestries that have hung there since the seventeenth century. One particularly gruesome panel showed Samson having his eyes gouged out. Since this was also Morris's bedroom one imagined it might have given him quite a few nightmares.

It seems that Dante Gabriel Rossetti was madly in love with Janey, Morris's wife. This caused a fair bit of friction in the household and Morris didn't take up proper residence until Rossetti stopped living there. There are numerous paintings of Janey around the house. She has that wonderfully droopy Victorian look with a long neck and abundantly flowing auburn hair.

The Morris legacy had been fiercely guarded by William's daughter May after he died. She never married but had a companion called Miss Lobb who was beefy enough to scare big old George Bernard Shaw when he came to tea one day. When May died, Miss Lobb took a bottle of brandy and a shotgun to bed with her and followed right along.

After seeing the house we were invited to visit the barns. One of them showed an exhibition of Morris's work and another contained a shop with museum quality artefacts from Morris's craftsman work.

Close by, there was another barn given over to supplying refreshments. We were served a delicious pot of tea, and sat drinking it and munching on lemon drizzle cake by the grassy banks of a small river that runs through the manor's gardens. William Morris sure knew how to live.

After tea, we strolled back to the boat and continued our travels towards Grafton Lock. Later, we found a picnic spot and scrambled up the bank onto a grass verge. An elegant swan joined us and waited patiently by our boat for bread crumbs as we spread out our meal on a red and white checked table cloth. We had Cambozola cheese, lamb sausages from Cutler and Bayliss the butcher in Lechlade, some celeriac from Mabys in Stowe, followed by blackberry and apple crumble that I had made from wild berries picked from the hedgerows. We also had some beer and home-made lavender lemonade.

After lunch I lay in the hot sun, watching a few clouds drifting overhead and lazily threw bread crumbs to the swan as Randall strummed his ukulele and sang *Life is Just a Bowl of Cherries*.

I was in heaven. Eventually we cleared up our picnic and went back to Stable Cottage. Then, at the end of our three weeks, it was with a deep sigh that we packed up and took ourselves back to our home in Los Angeles. There was no doubt about our decision, however, to look in earnest for a cottage to buy in the Cotswolds, although we would now have to wait until the next year before the search could begin.

Three

TINSEL TOWN, TROUT AND A THATCH
Burford, Windrush, Moreton-in-Marsh

Back in Los Angeles we started a cottage fund as the property prices in the Cotswolds were high and only climbing higher. I tried to stop buying shoes and Randy cut back on computer gadgets. These measures helped somewhat, but it was obvious that a bigger effort would be needed. I tried ways of increasing our income. We both earned good livings as actors, but there were plenty of times when we were 'resting'. My agent suggested that I do some public appearance work for corporate events and other such entertainments to earn extra money. This kind of work requires actors to impersonate historical figures and celebrities.

Because of my English accent, my agent thought I could work up an act as the Queen of England. I pointed out that I look nothing like our dear Queen and am quite a few decades younger. She said that prosthetic make-up would take care of that and dangled stories of how much money I could make were I to stick a *Mission Impossible*-type latex mask on my face and deck myself in a ball gown and jewels. She would market me as the royal Queen for the regal events and the comedy Queen for the fun ones.

Next, my agent had me check out a gathering of the performers who specialised in this impersonation work. These performers even have their own awards ceremony and one was coming up, so I went along.

Before the ceremony itself, there was a cocktail party, a wonderfully bizarre scene. There before me, squashed into a small bar, was a teeming throng of impersonators: three 'Abraham Lincolns' drinking martinis and a gaggle of 'Dolly Partons', oblivious to the fact that their combined boobs blocked everybody's way. Next to them were several 'Elizabeth Taylors' busily comparing outfits, while countless 'Elvises' swarmed among this motley crew. There was an authentic looking 'Austin Powers', who turned out to be a woman, and a drunk, lurching 'Mickey Rooney' propping up the bar. Holed up in another corner, making a mind-boggling tableau as they sat chatting were two 'Marilyn Monroes' in animated discussion with the 'Pope', 'Batman', 'Clark Gable', 'Betty Boop', 'W.C. Fields', and two 'Judy Garlands' – one male and one female.

For every impersonator who was vaguely recognisable, there were a dozen who were not. Three grey haired, balding men with beards puzzled me. When I asked who they were they answered in perfect unison, 'Sean Connery'. None of them looked even remotely like him. They must have had an inkling of this because, as if to compensate, they shouted lines from James Bond movies, their Scottish accents sounding like scalded cats being chased down an alley. Another guy, who was maybe five feet two inches tall, said he was 'Jimmy Stewart'. Wait a minute – wasn't Jimmy over six feet tall? A woman who was flat as a board said she was Mae West, and a man, with no resemblance whatsoever to Jerry Lewis, tried to get by with simply crossing his eyes and sticking out his front teeth. After a while, my brain began to melt as I tried to make it all work.

The drunk 'Mickey Rooney' had a crush on one of the performers playing 'Cher', though he hadn't figured out that this 'Cher' was being played by a man. Realising his mistake he moved on to a female 'Cher' who was in the process of singing *I've Got You Babe*. However, the fact that she was in the middle of a song didn't stop him from stumbling over to her, throwing his arm around her neck, and yelling down her microphone that they should 'get a room'.

It was all hilarious fun, but I couldn't see myself participating in any of this until my agent told me the actual figures that these actors earned. This information convinced me to sell my soul to the devil for the sake of the cottage fund.

My first job as a Queen impersonator was for a sales convention. I was booked as the comedy Queen and, in addition to my stick-on face; Randy had made me a two-dimensional corgi dog mounted on wheels that I could drag along behind me. Several other performers were booked to appear along with me. First on the bill was an actress who played a remarkably realistic 'Bette Davis'. She was supposed to do a scene from *Whatever Happened to Baby Jane*, but chaos reigned when her 'Joan Crawford' got stuck in traffic and couldn't make the performance in time.

At the last moment, Bette dragooned her six-foot-four-inch husband, who had driven her to the job, into standing in for Joan. He knew the lines from rehearsing with his wife, so he was flung into a wheelchair, covered with a blanket, and quickly fitted with a wig. A scarf hid his five-o-clock shadow and most of his face. He did a great job as a rather manly Joan. However, there were a few whispered comments, by audience members, about the depth of Joan's voice.

My act took the form of a question-and-answer session, and the MC asked a list of questions starting with, 'Your Majesty – what's in your handbag?' to which I replied, 'A list of people who ask me what's in my handbag.'

'Your Majesty, who does your hair?' he continued.

With great *hauteur* I answered, 'That's a very rude question but I'll tell you anyway. My hair is styled by the Royal Engineers and is designed to withstand a nuclear missile.' I then threw in a few jokes about there being so much malice at the palace that I had had to go in for a bit of Fergie Tossing. My big finish was a mock fight with the MC, ending in my chasing him around the stage handbagging (bashing) him senseless. Yes, I really had sold my soul to the devil.

But it was worth it. The cottage fund monies increased over the next year and we booked our same billet to rent for the following summer, this time for five weeks. I battled a terrible case of homesickness for most of the year, so I was very happy when we arrived in the Cotswolds the following June and took right up where we had left off. We immediately felt at home when our neighbours and the friends we had made in our small hamlet greeted us as if they had known us all our lives. It was great to hear the local butcher, Tony saying, 'Hello Mr and Mrs Montgomery. Has another year rolled round already?' as we stocked up on a new supply of lamb sausages and free-range chicken.

We knew from our previous visit that finding a cottage not only meant coming up with squillions in dough, but that finding one in just the right location would not be easy. We had also discovered that we would face stiff competition from all the weekenders who lived in London, rich retirees and executive business types who worked at a Honda plant in nearby Swindon. The cottage fund wasn't sufficient yet but we felt we should go ahead and view some cottages anyway. We registered with several estate agents and waited for them to show us what they had.

In the meantime, we were having such fun being back that we wanted to share our good times, so we invited our friends Pat and William to come and stay. They appeared the following Saturday with their dogs Bosun, an English bull terrier, and Bertie, a Jack Russell, in tow.

As we lived six thousand miles away in Los Angeles, word had not reached us of Bosun's shenanigans. Apparently, Pat and William found it necessary to stuff their pockets with money every time they took him for a walk in order to pay off the people whose lives were affected by his outrageous behaviour. A typical Bosun trick might be to spy a victim during his outing and lurch at them, dragging William along for the ride. This would usually be some poor fellow innocently eating fish and chips on a park bench. Suddenly his meal would be whisked away by the greedy Bosun, who would then swallow the whole lot, including a piece of cod, chips, a pickle and several pages of the Daily Mail.

Bosun had the smallest brain of any canine ever born. We took a flash photo of him once, and a full minute and a half later he blinked. On another occasion, he ran at high speed into a brick wall. We thought he would keel over dead; however, he rebounded from the wall and, after a slight pause, shuffled off to his water dish and lapped away as if nothing had happened.

We set off for a hike near Moreton-in-Marsh with Pat, William and the dogs as soon as they arrived, stopping in Burford for lunch on the way. This interesting town on the River Windrush was the site of a fortified river ford in Anglo-Saxon times.

The Windrush begins its southward journey near Temple Guiting and meanders through Lower Slaughter and Bourton-on-the Water before flowing on to the Barringtons. The Windrush provides exhilarating river walks through Swinbrook and Asthall, once the home of the famous Mitford family, and on to Minster Lovell. This village is known for its impressive ruined abbey which was built in the fifteenth century. Minster Lovell is the Windrush's final riverside settlement before it reaches Witney and continues on to meet the Thames near Oxford.

The lovely Windrush certainly enhances Burford, which became an important crossroads and a wealthy wool town during medieval times. It is an interesting contrast to the surrounding villages with their narrow twisting lanes, as the main street has a broad sweep of cobbles and grass in front of its ancient cottages and shops. These are little changed from Tudor times, and Randy grabbed his camera when he saw the wonderfully off-centre angles of the beams and window frames.

We strolled around and visited the magnificent fifteenth century parish church of St John the Baptist, another example of past riches based on wool. Next we did a quick tour of the seventeenth century Burford House Hotel, which is well worth a visit. We continued along the High Street that's filled with boutiques, pubs, restaurants and antique shops, and stopped at a bygones store called The George. This building was once a coaching inn during Tudor times and its owner gave us a tour of various historic features before we shopped there for old maps. The basement is delightfully spooky with its huge beams and seems to have remained unchanged since it was built five or six hundred years ago. There is a poem scratched on the glass of an upstairs window that is attributed to Samuel Pepys, the diarist who lived there for a time.

After this, we ambled down the side streets and Randy, who loves lamb, wanted to have lunch in the fifteenth century Lamb Inn, especially when he saw that it was located on Sheep Street. A sudden chilly rain shower sent us scurrying inside. We oohed and aahed over the ancient flagstone floors and ship's beams as we passed through a jolly bar to a series of cosy lounges that lay behind. They looked to be fashioned from several cottages strung together. Here it was peaceful and quiet with wingback armchairs and comfy sofas surrounding a blazing log fire. We snuggled in the down pillows of the sofas and ordered a light lunch from a selection that included a bacon and brie salad and Dover sole.

As Randall and William went to fetch our drinks, I was suddenly struck by a long forgotten memory from my childhood. I realised that the Lamb Inn was a perfect example of those old fashioned hotels that my parents took me to for our family vacations where it always seemed to be raining and the guests were mostly elderly. Many of the guests lived in these hotels permanently and did nothing all day but sleep, read the newspapers and play bridge.

My brother and I would mooch around the hotel, looking out at the driving rain and would usually end up playing ping pong in the basement. Upstairs, meanwhile, the resident guests would wait with keen anticipation for the arrival of the next meal which was routinely four or five courses and eaten in hushed Victorian primness in the echoing dining room. Typically, lunch would start with Mulligatawny soup and go on to a fish course, usually shrimp cocktail. This would be followed by lamb chops and boiled new potatoes. Roly-poly pudding or spotted dick would be served up next, followed by biscuits, cheese and coffee. The guests would often demand a second helping of dessert and stagger away from the lunch table, just making it to the armchairs in the lounge before collapsing.

They would finish reading that morning's newspapers and vicious arguments would break out about the crossword clues in The Times. Often, walking canes would be raised in anger. But then, slowly, almost imperceptibly, the rustling of the newspapers would die down and the chatting would fade away. Heads would nod and loll as, one by one, the guests fell asleep. At first the dead silence and all the prone bodies made the lounge look like there had been a First World War mustard gas attack but gradually a cacophony of snarks, snores and whistles would build to a see-saw climax.

At about four o'clock, way, way off in the distance, the barely discernable tinkling and rattling of china would be heard as the tea trolley approached. Snuffling and sputtering, the old codgers would rouse themselves from their slumber. Newspapers would be thrown down with mutters of, 'Ah, tea at last,' or, 'Goodness, I must have dropped off.' As soon as the tea trolley crossed the threshold, canes and crutches would be cast aside in a spirited dash to grab the best tea cakes, causing scuffles to break out and harsh words to be exchanged. The odd iced cupcake might be ripped in half before the dust settled. Threats and accusations would give way to a feeding frenzy over fish paste sandwiches, Bakewell tart and strawberry sponge cake. Then, slowly, everybody would settle down again until the dinner gong sounded an hour or so later.

As we finished lunch, the skies cleared and by the time we reached our destination, Batsford Deer Park, which is a couple of miles outside Moreton-in-Marsh, the sun was shining. Batsford was part of a sheep-rearing estate given in the eighth century by the King of Mercia to the Bishop of Worcester, who later lost part of it to a greedy nobleman called Ethelred the Unready. Randy, the wag, loved these ancient English noblemen names and wondered if there had also been a Hector the Hysterical or Igor the Incontinent.

The hike started in the middle of Moreton-in-Marsh High Street, just a few feet above the ancient Roman

Fosse Way. We strolled along Corder's Lane and our walking guide told us to go through the first of eleven kissing-gates. I had visions of pushing through crowds of the local villagers making loud smacking sounds as they rolled around in steamy embraces at every gate. In fact, these gates, built on a pivot, are shaped to allow only one person through at a time in order to stop cattle escaping. They get their name because, traditionally, when couples use them, the man is supposed to receive a kiss from the woman after he ushers her through. A few more kissing gates later, we could just see Batsford House over the hedges. This Palladian mansion, built by Thomas Edwards Freeman, was replaced in the late 1880s by the present Victorian Tudor-Gothic house that is well known for its arboretum. The Mitford family, ancestors of the famous Mitford sisters, took the additional name of Freeman and held the estate until 1919 when it was sold to Lord Dulverton. The Mitford children were reputedly hunted in these fields by their eccentric father, Lord Redesdale. Apparently the children were substituted for the fox, when one was not to be found, and I had a vision of them running, squealing off into the distance as their father chased them on horseback with a pack of hounds. Fortunately, they all survived to adulthood.

We took a circular walk on a public footpath and really enjoyed spotting the deer in Batsford Deer Park before they bolted nervously away. We were able to take a good look, with our binoculars, at the rather ugly Victorian pile that had housed the Mitford family before they took off to live in their next house in Asthall near Burford. There is also a Falconry Centre nearby and, as our friends Pat and William are avid bird watchers, they were thrilled to see these birds being exercised.

We then took a detour to Batsford Church, a Norman-Victorian gem, which is beautifully situated on steeply rising ground near the entrance of Batsford Park. The stained-glass windows in the church dating from 1888 are wonderfully overdone. Their designer, C.E. Kempe, was known for his use of elaborately patterned curtains and hangings and the stained glass in the east window has all the bells and whistles he could possibly jam in.

During the hike, we came across a farmer repairing a dry stone wall. These walls are characteristic of the Cotswold region and add enormously to the beauty of the landscape. Made from the local honey-coloured stone without any kind of mortar, they are assembled like giant jigsaw puzzles. We watched, fascinated, as the farmer took pieces of jagged, uneven stone and fitted them together perfectly as he talked. I asked how he did it so expertly.

St Nicholas' Church, Oddington

'Mainly by feel,' he answered in his broad country accent. He was a great old character and he gave a terrific impromptu talk on dry stone walling.

'Its limestone, see, and we gather the stones from all around when we rebuild like this. After you do it for a while, you even know where the stones come from by their colour. See this one in my hand? Now that's from Guiting, and that one – that's from Oddington. These walls don't just divide the fields; they provide shelter for small birds, toads, frogs and insects. They have all sorts growing in between the stones too. Wild flowers, herbs, berries – you name it. Why, I wouldn't be surprised if there weren't a few Roman coins in there too.'

He told us that until recently this craft had been dying out. Now, however, farmers are given grants to rebuild. The National Trust, together with the Dry Walling Association and Stroud College, provide a course for those wanting to learn this craft along with others like roof thatching and stone conservation. When we finally buy our cottage, I thought, I am going to take the dry walling course myself as I can't bear to think of these wonderful old crafts being lost.

Near the end of our walk, which took in a Roman fort situated near the Moreton Showground, William elected to continue hiking with the dogs while we took off in the car to shop for a few items needed for the evening meal. When we arrived in town, Randy went to find some good wine while Pat and I shopped in the small supermarket. William, on his way to meet us, had not put the dogs on a leash and Bosun, obviously on the lookout for ways to retain his title of 'Stupidest Dog on the Planet', had fallen into a stagnant ditch filled with dank water and rotting vegetation. Bosun sank like a stone, turning over in the water as he did so until his four legs stuck straight up in the air. He made no attempt to save himself and Bertie bravely splashed in after him. William then jumped in to save them both. He dragged the dogs out and came to find us, soaking wet, trailing reeds, mud and stinking algae. He arrived looking like a fugitive from *The Zombie*

Bogman of Hideous Creek horror movie. Naturally, the supermarket manager refused to let him in the shop.

Blithely oblivious, inside the supermarket, Pat and I were drifting around the aisles shopping, yakking and failing to notice William outside frantically waving and rapping on the shop window. We were totally immersed in our usual habit of discussing different weight-loss diets as we filled our baskets with Devonshire double-cream cakes, full-fat ice cream and over-ripe Brie cheese. After a time, we came out of the shop and found William surrounded by a crowd of local kids, who jeered and pointed as he made grotesque horror-movie faces and threw handfuls of pond muck at them.

We took poor William home, hosed him off and cheered him up by serving him a dinner of trout, from a local organic fish farm, stuffed with garlic, fennel and shallots and finished off with a *beurre-blanc* sauce. We had gathered some pick-your-own asparagus on our way home and added this to the trout, along with caramelised sweet-potato puree, washing it all down with an impudent little rosé from the Rhône region of France. This was followed by a dessert, from a recipe I had brought over from America, for pistachio *crème anglais* and an Armagnac prune soufflé which tasted divine.

After dinner, we amused ourselves by telling true stories about our relatives, vying for the most outrageous. My story about my Great Uncle Arthur's activities during the Second World War was the winner. Great Uncle Arthur was unfit for active service and had been given a desk job. He was in charge of assigning thousands of new recruits to various training camps around Britain. One of these camps on a Scottish island required five hundred new soldiers to be sent there. Great Uncle Arthur, wag that he was, selected every recruit named Smith or Smythe. I tried to imagine a drill sergeant bawling out a new recruit with 'Smith, come here!' and five hundred men would step forward.

The next morning, we all sat around having breakfast in the garden while I regaled our friends with more snippets from the wonderfully entertaining English newspapers. Before doing so, however, I translated some of the code phrases that crop up regularly, so that Randy could understand them. When the papers report upon someone's *unbuttoned style* this means this person is actually as drunk as a lord. If a big mucky muck in the news resigns from his high-profile position to *spend more time with his family*, he has, in fact, just been fired. When an aristocrat is referred to in the news as *otherworldly*, he or she is mad as a March hare, and if a suspect is *helping the police with their enquiries* that person is usually being interrogated to the third degree. *Brenda* is the code name (coined by the satirical magazine *Private Eye*) for the Queen of England, and a *love nest* is a euphemism for a house that has been bought by a Member of Parliament for his mistress.

My snippet this time was about a mishap that had befallen a typical family with teenage children. Apparently, the parents of this particular teenager had left him alone in the house for the first time, while they took a brief holiday in Scotland after making him promise not to wreck the house with any big parties. Shortly after the parents departed, their son left a laundry basket full of washing on the stove. Just why he chose to do this was never explained. Later, as he rushed out to meet his mates, he inadvertently brushed up against the stove's 'on' switch. This caused the basket of laundry to catch fire, consequently igniting a deodorant canister in a bag of groceries nearby, setting off an explosion that demolished the kitchen, reducing it to a charred cinder, and actually raising the roof of the house several feet. When the roof settled back down, there was a foot-wide crack the entire length of the front wall. Imagine what would have happened if this kid had actually thrown a party. He might have decimated the entire neighbourhood.

Next, I looked in the local newspaper for cottages for sale; I tossed the paper away in disgust as there was nothing in our price range. A few moments later our estate agent called with a cottage for us to view − immediately if we wanted. The cottage was, with a stretch, just in our price range so Pat, William, Randy and I jumped in our car and tore off to a small village in the southern Cotswolds.

Maureen, the agent, was waiting to show us around when we arrived. After she unlocked the front door, we all stepped inside and found ourselves in the smallest room I had ever seen, outside of my childhood dollhouse. The four of us and the agent filled up the entire living room. The furniture consisted of two small chairs and a table that held a minute television. Maureen acted as if it was quite normal for us all to be jammed in the living room tighter than the passengers on the Underground in rush hour.

'As you can see the living room is very light and bright,' she said perkily. 'Now, if you could all just step into the kitchen, I'll be able to close the front door.' We all shuffled together in a line and squeezed into the kitchen, which was even smaller.

'Wow! This is tiny,' said my friend Pat. 'Was this a barn conversion?'

Maureen looked evasive and muttered, 'Not exactly.'

She led us upstairs to a landing that was the size of a postage stamp and threw open a door as if it were the ballroom at Buckingham Palace.

'Oh good, a walk-in closet,' said Randy.

Maureen replied, 'Er... no... that's the master bedroom.'

I tried for a positive spin as I looked out of the bedroom window. 'Well the view is nice anyway. This seems to be in the grounds of that bigger cottage next door.'

Maureen replied, 'Yes, that's Victory Cottage. Years ago it used to be the Victory pub.'

'So this building must have been one of the outbuildings of the pub. Which one?' I asked.

Maureen ignored my question and tried to herd us into the second bedroom. This was impossible because it was completely filled with a single bed. Randy said, 'Was this cottage once a storage shed?'

Maureen looked shifty. 'Not exactly... shall we look at the garden?'

Randy interrupted her. 'No, wait. I want to get to the bottom of this.'

Suddenly a light bulb went on in my head. 'Randy,' I said, 'I think you just have. I bet this was the pub toilet.'

'No!' exclaimed everybody, bursting into laughter. But it was obvious from the look on Maureen's face that it was and she gave a frosty reply.

'We prefer the word *convenience*.'

'So this is a convenience conversion?' quipped Randy.

Maureen countered defensively, 'Well, the walls are the original Cotswold stone and it's perfectly habitable now as you can see.'

Randy then asked, 'Is the address of this cottage Number Two Brown Lane?'

Maureen glowered as Pat stifled her giggles enough to say, 'If you buy it, you could call it Dun Groan'in.'

William chimed in with a few alternatives, 'Or Two Seater Hall, or wait a minute, what about Poo Loo or perhaps Pisser's Rest?'

Then we tried to top each other with one pun after another.

'S Bend Chalet.'

'Maison Merde.'

'Spend-a-Penny Cottage.'

By now Maureen's face was reddening with suppressed rage and she asked, 'Do you actually have any interest in this cottage?'

Randy replied through tears of laughter, 'I'm sorry, but... no.'

'I think we had better leave,' I said, 'Maureen is looking a little flushed.'

As we made a rapid exit Randy muttered, 'No s—t.'

From this experience, we realised that the purchase price of Cotswold cottages had risen so alarmingly that even a remodelled pub toilet was now almost out of our range. In the news, we were seeing that television stars and multimillionaire super models were rapidly buying up most of the available cottages. All this seemed to make it well nigh impossible for us to achieve our goal. Randy and I decided it was time to regroup and rethink – we would have to pull something out of the hat.

The Thames near Buscot

Four

FUNDING THE DREAM
Bibury, Kemble, River Thames

The plane lifted off from Heathrow – taking us back to Los Angeles – and, as I stared out of the window at the green patchwork fields of England getting smaller by the second, I was overcome with sadness. Dear little England was quickly disappearing beneath the clouds. To console myself, I savoured the memory of a terrific outing from a week or so earlier. We had been taken on an interesting jaunt by a wonderful local character; I shall call him Bob. He was a salty old boy who made us laugh with his sardonic take on the inhabitants of the villages.

'Have you noticed what happens when it rains a lot in one of the smaller lanes in our village?'

'No, I can't say I have,' I replied.

'Old Mrs M., from Tinker's cottage, is so nervous about missing the morning bus that she rises at dawn to catch it. By the time the bus arrives her Wellington boots have sunk into the mud and she has to climb on board without them. She leaves them there until she returns with her shopping in the late afternoon, puts them back on, digs herself out and toddles off home.'

He knew all the gossip from the southern Cotswold villages stretching back for decades. On this day, Bob had taken us to Bibury, described by the artist William Morris as the most beautiful village in England and its setting in an idyllic valley on the banks of the sparkling, trout-laden River Coln certainly validates his statement. An elegant eighteenth century bridge leads across the Coln to Arlington Row, the most photographed row of cottages in the Cotswolds. These buildings were used for wool storage in medieval times and were converted during the seventeenth century into dwellings to house the wool weavers who supplied Arlington Mill. Rack Isle, the grass sward in front of Arlington Row was once used by the workers for drying out their wool.

Bibury boasts several other attractions including The Swan Hotel, Bibury Trout Farm where customers can catch their own trout and Arlington Mill complete with its very own ghost. Though this part of Bibury was very interesting there were too many tourists around for my taste so we quickly moved on to a splendid lunch in nearby Bibury Court, a grand Jacobean country manor house that has now been converted into a hotel and restaurant.

It was a perfect, sunny day, and we were astonished at the beauty of Bibury Court, which is set in six acres of wild gardens and has about forty rooms. Its architecture appeared to be largely unchanged since it was built in 1633 by Sir Thomas Sackville, a knight and gentleman usher to King James I.

We were seated for lunch in an ancient conservatory with a sweeping view of the lush gardens and a stream that meandered through the grounds. This stream is, in fact, the river Coln and several Bibury Court hotel guests could be seen contentedly fishing for trout on its banks.

Bob insisted we have a leisurely three-course lunch, which was fine with us. In fact, we had missed breakfast in preparation, knowing that this treat was in store.

'Come along you two – don't hold back – neither of you is bigger than a bar of soap,' said Bob.

'Thanks, well in that case I'll have *escabeche* of Cornish Red Mullet,' I said.

'I'll go for the linguini of Scottish *girolles* with parmesan and thyme.'

'Jolly good choice, Randall, I feel like all fish today, so I'm having the Cornish squid... ooh, look what it comes with... risotto of lemon and a toasted brioche topped with *foie gras*, fig and apple chutney. Let us see, to follow I'll have the caramelised Scottish halibut with the ragout of wild Fowey mussels. Now what about you two?' said Bob.

'Hmm,' said Randy, 'fish sounds good. I'll have the roast Bibury trout; I like the sound of that. They probably fished it right out of the stream outside, and it comes with leeks, bacon, crayfish and summer truffle.'

'Well, I can't resist the Broadfield Farm beef with yummy braised red cabbage and parsley creamed potato,' I said.

In between courses, a chatty waiter told us a story, appropriately about Bibury Court.

'In the 1930s,' he said, 'before it was a hotel, Bibury Court belonged to a titled lady. She was widowed and lived in massive Bibury Court alone except for one servant – her butler. When she was at dinner and ready for the next course, she would call up the local telephone operator and tell her to ring back to Bibury Court. The butler would then answer from the kitchen and the telephone operator would pass on the message from his mistress for him to serve up the next course in the dining room.'

By this time our entrées were history and we were now onto our desserts: crème caramel with roast Cox's orange pippin apples and cider raisins, *tarte tatin* and a mixture of sorbets. After lunch, we had coffee in the oak-panelled drawing room where, despite the warm day, logs burned brightly in the fireplace. The hotel owners have cleverly kept everything in the style of an ancient country house and we were very comfortable lolling about on the big squishy sofas.

Next, we meandered through the grounds and discovered that a gate in one of the walled gardens opened onto a path that led to St Mary's Church, only a few yards away. We strolled along it and walked through the gate to explore the church. The earliest mention of this building is AD 721 when it was a Saxon church of great size. When the Normans came along, they usually razed these Saxon churches to the ground and built on top of them. However, St Mary's is of special interest because a great deal of the original Saxon church remains. What the Normans did at this time amounted to a sort of 'Design on a Dime' remodel, merely lopping off the upper half of the church and rebuilding the tops of the windows and the tower in their own style. I was fascinated to see that a Saxon gravestone had been saved by being brought into the church. It is carved in the

Scandinavian Saxon style with interlacing circles and pellets and is well worth a look.

So, too, is a panel of thirteenth century Grisaille stained glass in the south window of the sanctuary. St Mary's, despite its earlier makeover, has not been changed since the fourteenth century and has escaped the typically ugly Victorian refit.

After this, we returned to Bibury Court's grounds and finished off our visit by strolling alongside the trout stream and watching the antics of a dozen or so ducks waddling in and out of the water.

I came out of my reverie on the plane and couldn't believe that I was sighing with nostalgia over my memories with England still in view. Both Randy and I were sad. We seemed to be leaving too soon this time. In a way, I was pleased. I was sure, the sadder I felt, the more incentive it would give me to find a way to buy our cottage.

As the plane flew higher and England gradually disappeared under the clouds, I brought out my sheaf of English newspapers. This was another way to make the trip last a little longer, as they could always be counted on for a few amusing stories. They didn't disappoint. I read out one of the news stories to Randy. It sounded like a comedy sketch, but apparently was a report of a true event. It told of a therapist who had been accused of taking advantage of a patient with a split personality by persuading one of her alter egos to become his mistress, another to work as his cleaner and a third to give him money for his vacation. It was unclear how this patient had become suspicious of her treatment, but she eventually confronted the therapist. He told her he would not discuss the matter because he had a duty of confidentiality to his patients which included all her other personalities.

Another piece caught my eye, concerning a woman who after entering a cake competition had won second place. She was quite pleased, until she discovered that she was the only person who had entered the competition!

Our spirits were low after we got back to Los Angeles as reality set in. We needed a new plan to achieve our dream of buying a cottage – but couldn't think of one.

I decided a visit to my therapist Sara was in order. My 'shrink' is a very wise woman.

'How do you think you are going to acquire a cottage?' she asked.

'By earning as much money as I can and saving every penny,' I replied.

'Why don't you add this into the equation?' she asked, 'If you "act as if", you will reach your goal much sooner.'

'I don't understand,' I said.

'Pretend you're already in a position to shop for a cottage and start viewing them. When you do this, the necessary money will manifest itself in your life.'

I took this idea home to Randy and we put it into action. We signed up with additional estate agents in England and had them send particulars of cottages for sale.

Next, we logged on to an email site that advertises country and cottage homes for sale from all over England – it's called *Prime Location*. We had a lot of fun with this – almost every day, it seemed, a new batch of cottages would appear via email.

We would print up the specs and discuss their various pros and cons as if we were about to make an offer. Soon we saw a very attractive cottage for sale, in our price range, in the village of Kemble. We were excited, but couldn't understand why it was so inexpensive until we called up our friends, Sandra and Jim, in the Cotswolds and asked them if they would go and look at this cottage for us.

'You want us to view a cottage for you in Kemble?' said Sandra, sounding surprised.

Randy and I looked this village up on *Google Earth* and as we pulled back from it to view the surrounding countryside, we both realized that the cottage we had in mind was actually on the runway of a military airfield. Not next to it or nearby, but on the runway, at the end. The occupant of that cottage could wink at the pilot as eye contact could easily be made during take-off. We had identified the tragic flaw of this potential home.

To be fair to the village of Kemble it is noted for its Bristol Aero collection in its museum. This collection exhibits over ninety years of Bristol Aviation and Space Heritage and has a limited opening time from April to October.

The tragic flaws, or TFs as we called them from then on, became more obvious to us as we received further specifications and particulars. Among the photos of the cottages, the measurements of the rooms, the number of bedrooms and bathrooms and the actual location, we would quickly be able to figure out if a cottage fit the bill.

The more we looked at the cottages on this website the more defined and specific our requirements became. It was a good education and we realised that there were a lot of subtleties to take into consideration before we could make our choice. Interesting conclusions began to emerge. To begin with, something I had never thought of before gradually made itself apparent – that the location of the cottage is just as important as the cottage itself.

The village in which a cottage is situated and the proximity of that village to various desired amenities is extremely important. Many things come into play, such as the cottage's proximity to any source of noise, its orientation to the sun rising and setting and so on. Several of the cottages we viewed on *Prime Location* were right on a road with almost no frontage. Of course when they were built, mostly in the seventeenth century, these roads were cart tracks, so traffic noise was negligible, but now it was a major issue and to be right on a road, even a country lane, with cars driving within a foot or so of the front door, would not be very pleasant.

Many cottages didn't have much of a front garden and even less land in the back. Most of the smaller houses had been farm labourers' cottages and they belonged to the feudal lord of the manor, therefore, no extra land had been included. Sometimes several farm workers' houses had been built in a block of three or four semi-detached buildings. These were often at right angles to the road, and at most, had only a tiny communal garden.

Another consideration is a cottage's location in relation to a village. Some cottages are situated in isolated farmland with no other houses around. I knew I didn't want that. Others are squashed in the middle of a village, completely surrounded by other cottages, with only postage stamp sized yards. This wouldn't work either. I wanted to be on the outskirts of a village or hamlet, hopefully with a view of the fields.

Also, I didn't want to live in what we called a 'wrinkly' village where everyone was retired and doddery. Neither did I want to be in a village populated almost solely by weekenders and therefore deserted during the week. The ideal village should have a pub that serves good food, and if possible, a village shop. Also, a village with a church is considered a great asset, as is one with a school.

We studied every cottage that appeared on *Prime Location* and then sought out where they were on *Google Earth*. After a while, we realised that we were probably asking for the impossible. But heck, we were asking for the impossible anyway because we just didn't have the money to make a purchase happen.

Gloom lowered over us in a major way. This was good actually, as it made us realise that we really wanted this cottage in the Cotswolds. I had always known it wasn't going to be easy. Hoping to renew our resolve, I decided to write a pros and cons list that would determine whether the Herculean effort needed to make this happen was worth it.

Randy helped me and it took several days of really thinking hard to complete it. At first the cons column was predominant, but then, gradually, the pros column pushed into the lead and I felt a huge relief. Whatever the effort, it was going to be worth it. But how could I get to my goal?

I sat down for a think. I had quite happily acquired my mother's dream of getting a cottage, so I tried to imagine, if she were here, exactly what she would do right now. It came to me right away. She would have a cup of tea. Whenever she was stuck with a problem, a nice big jolt of caffeine was always first on the agenda.

My mother could not have survived for very long without a strong cuppa. She would boil a kettle of water and pour it onto a heap of loose tea leaves piled onto the already existing sludge at the bottom of the teapot. She would then stir this gunk with a spoon, somewhat like dredging a pond. Finally, she would pour herself a steaming cup of char. The tea was so strong it could easily have been used to strip a car engine and the inside of the teapot looked like furred-up plumbing. Often, the spoon used to stir this slurry would actually stand upright by itself.

It took gallons of this concoction to get Mum going in the morning, and somewhere between throwing down the fifth or sixth cup she would start muttering groggily under her breath, 'I'm coming round', sounding as if she had just been KO'd after going ten rounds in a prize fight. There would be a few more cups at breakfast and all would be well for an hour or so, but, by eleven o'clock in the morning, she would suddenly sway and clutch onto a piece of furniture as if she were about to fall unconscious on the ground. Staggering over to a wall, she would slowly slide down it, her hands desperately scrabbling for anything to stop her slow sink to the floor. If she happened to be standing near someone at the time she would grab his or her arm and exclaim in a voice worthy of Sarah Bernhardt, 'Ohhhh... I'm gasping. Quick! Put the kettle on!'

Although the teapot would be almost completely full of sodden leaves by late afternoon, Mum would cram in another heaping of fresh tea and, after adding boiling water, would stir the pot's Stygian depths and pour the tea, like treacle, into our cups. After this ritual was complete, all of the women in the family would huddle around the kitchen table like a coven of witches, the steam from the tea billowing around us, and discuss the nature of our problem.

I staged a re-enactment of my mother's tea-making technique, and drank a cup of the yucky, viscous brew straight down. Wow! Firecrackers exploded in my head, the scrambled neurons in my frontal lobe almost knocking me unconscious. I hadn't had this much caffeine since I could remember. Pulling myself together with a supreme effort of will, I immediately applied my turbo-charged brains to the problem at hand.

Now, how would Mum see it? I tried to channel her. Yes, she would ask questions such as:

'What are your assets?'

'Well, we own a house here in Los Angeles – or more correctly – the bank owns the house until the mortgage is paid.'

'How can you exploit it?'

'I dunno... er... er... rent it out for a film shoot maybe... Whoa!'

This was a great idea. I couldn't imagine why I hadn't thought of it before. My shrink Sara had been right. Acting "as if" was already producing results. Our house is near several movie studios, and I had often noticed film trucks unloading movie equipment into nearby homes. Although I knew our house couldn't compete with the larger mansions, our living room did have a high ceiling, a prerequisite for any kind of filming.

I got in touch with several film-location companies, and Randy set to work taking photographs of the house and emailing them. After a visit from a couple of location scouts, we were told that our house could be suitable for smaller independent films, commercial shoots and infomercials. We signed up and hoped.

Before too long, we received an offer from a location company for a one-day shoot on an independent short film. I didn't ask to see the script – I didn't care; I was happy that the money earned from this would be adding to the cottage fund.

The shoot was scheduled for the following month and, in the meantime, I looked around for further inspiration. When none came, I tried some more caffeine jolts to jumpstart another money making idea. However, I found I had to retire the tea pot for the time being because of the insomnia it induced and the way I looked as a result. My image in the mirror resembled a cross between the staring-eyed runaway bride and a female Popeye.

I switched to decaf and managed to get focused without any extra stimulation. The word 'assets' began running around my mind. What else did I have? I made what turned out to be a distressingly short list. On it were the plays I had written with my comedy group. I had often thought about putting together a college and theatre tour of them but, as it was such a big undertaking, I had always shied away at the last minute. Now I had some real incentive. It would be hard work and perhaps risky but could garner me another nice chunk of money for the cottage fund.

I put together a business plan and worked hard setting up tour dates. My research showed that I would do well to start with a booking at a college that was known for its conservative taste. If this college booked me all the other colleges would fall in line because they would know that I had been thoroughly checked out. The college I had in mind booked only family fare, but since this was the nature of my shows there was no problem there. However, the artistic director, whom I shall call Mr Morris, wanted to meet me and make sure that I was squeaky clean before a contract would be signed. We made a plan for him to come to my home office to finalise the arrangements the next time he was in town.

By now the date for the location filming at our house had rolled around and Randy and I gave over our living room and kitchen to the film crew. As the crew laid endless cables and set up lights I retreated to my office at the back of the house.

Pretty soon I had a call from Mr. Morris saying he was in town, close by, and we agreed he could come by in the next ten minutes to discuss our arrangements. A short time later Randy came into the office with a worried look on his face.

'Did you know they're filming porno in the living room?'

'What?! My college guy is almost here!'

I ran out into the living room and over to the front door which was propped open by a pile of cables snaking through it. As I yanked the door open, I saw Mr Morris starting up the front path.

'Hello there!' I sang out.

Dashing out of the door to head him off, I tripped on one of the film cables, and did such a spectacular somersaulting fall that two people on the sidewalk stopped and applauded. Luckily, I landed on the lawn, so no harm was done.

Mr Morris stopped dead in his tracks his mouth agape. I scrambled to my feet thinking quickly.

'How did you like that?' I said. 'I thought I would show you some of the physical comedy I do in my show.'

He was speechless, but obviously quite impressed.

'Eh, we've got a film shoot going on in the house... come this way.'

I quickly led him to the back of the house before he saw what was going on in the living room. When we got there, the kitchen door had been blocked shut for the shoot and the only other door led back into the living room. I kept Mr Morris talking while Randy got a ladder from the garage, and we then persuaded him to climb in through the office window. In spite of the chaos, our meeting went well, ending with the promise of a contract.

We heaved a sigh of relief as Mr. Morris climbed back down the ladder on his way out. Just as he reached the last rung a crew member came over and in a booming voice said, 'The director wants to know if we can film in your bathroom for the nude, wife-swap scene.'

Well, the college part of the tour didn't work out so well, but I managed to book some local theatres instead. Shortly before we set off on tour a letter arrived from our friends Pat and William in England. As I opened the envelope a stack of pictures fell out and fluttered to the floor. The first image showed their dog Bosun once again up to no good. In the photo he was tearing along with his leash still attached to a set of heavy wooden steps that belonged to Pat and William's holiday caravan. He had been tied to these to secure him but now these steps were being dragged along behind him, bumping and splintering into shards, as he gave chase to some unseen temptation in the distance.

The next set of photos plunged me into a well of nostalgia and homesickness as they showed shots of all of us on a trip we had taken on the river near the source of the Thames on our last trip to the Cotswolds. The Thames is the longest river in England and flows into the North Sea at the Thames estuary. It covers a large portion of South Eastern and Western England and it is fed by more than 20 tributaries. So many historic events have taken place on the River Thames and its banks and bridges that is justly earns its description of "Liquid History" by John Burns. This river is now a major leisure attraction that includes rowing, sailing, kayaking, punting and long boating among its pleasures. Randy had rented a cabin cruiser so that all four of us could spend a weekend boating. He was gung ho for making this journey into a sort of camping trip on water, and had spent quite a bit of time planning and shopping for meals we could cook in the boat's tiny galley, as well as getting together all the things needed for a two-night trip. Randy enjoyed overloading the boat with food, his ukulele, other musical instruments, and a sound system. Despite this he also intended to stop for meals along the way.

The weekend we had chosen started out idyllically with a light, soft breeze and pleasant sunny spells. Randy and William took turns playing skipper, while Pat and I perched on top of the cabin cruiser and enjoyed the terrific views of the rolling Cotswolds hills, dotted with sheep. We cooked a meal in the galley in the evening and joked and laughed until it was time for bed. I am a one for my comfort and I was already lamenting not having my hair dryer for the morning, so I wasn't looking forward to bedding down in the cramped bunks. Nevertheless, I managed to fall asleep quite easily. Only an hour later, though, I was awoken by the light rain that was falling. It had found a way through the hatch above me and was splashing on my forehead, one drip at a time.

In the morning, despite Randy's attempt to provision us with enough stores to cross the Atlantic, we somehow had no butter for toast. But he discouraged us from stopping to get some, as we were behind schedule for our dinner reservations that evening. I could see why, as the boat seemed to move more slowly than hikers walking along the towpath next to us.

We almost made it to our destination before the clouds turned black and the heavens opened to the accompaniment of rolling thunder. The downpour portrayed in *Singin' in the Rain* seemed like a mere drizzle next to the intensity of this cloudburst.

Pat and I left the guys happily steering the boat, and scrambled down to the lower cabin to make some hot tea. I was sitting drinking mine when a thunderclap exploded immediately overhead. It was so loud that I jumped out of my skin, causing the tea I was drinking to shoot up out of my cup, hit the low cabin ceiling and come back down all over my head. Pat had captured this on film and, there among the photos, was one of me wearing my cup of tea.

By the time we finally made it to our dinner destination, a gastro-pub charmingly called the Trout at Tadpole Bridge, the storm had passed. The Trout is on the river near the town of Bampton, serves the best food for miles around and is particularly well known for its fresh seafood. Some diners make the round trip from as far away as London for lunch or an evening meal. It's very popular and we had to make our reservation on time or lose our table. We made it with two minutes to spare, and it was fun to arrive by boat, walk through the pub gardens and hang out at the bar for a drink as we took our time looking over the menu. That evening, Randy and I shared a dish of *moules*, which were some of the best I have ever eaten. They were cooked in a perfectly-balanced Thai curry sauce, and we followed that dish with fresh skate wing that had been lightly battered. Pat and William had excellent Dover sole and duck *confit*.

After this, we went back to the boat and drifted down the river for a while before tying up for the night. Randy and I were celebrating our wedding anniversary, so we slipped away for a romantic walk along the towpath to nearby Radcot Lock. The river was bathed in the light of a full moon, and the deserted lock looked eerily serene surrounded by its weeping willow trees, perfectly reflected in the glass-like stillness of the water. We stood for a long time on the lock bridge enjoying the silence. Eventually, we sauntered back to the boat, still revelling in the brilliant moonlight, and talked about how fortunate we were to be here in the Cotswolds.

In Pat and William's letter, which accompanied the photos of our trip together, they told of a cottage soon to be for sale in the small village of Filkins, located in the southern part of the Cotswolds. In the photo Pat had included of this property this cottage appeared to have been built in the seventeenth century using ships' beams. Around this time, ships that had been captured from the Spanish armada were often dismantled, and their beams reused to build workers' homes. Many of these beams were prized for their elaborate carvings made by sailors to while away the many months at sea.

We were thrilled to have a lead on this cottage that might be coming up for sale around the time we would be returning to England for our summer holiday. This news gave me renewed enthusiasm to earn more for the cottage fund, and I set off for my theatre tour with a lot more hope. I had booked several dates in Southern California, and they all went remarkably well. I enjoyed performing for the audiences who laughed long and loud and there were no major problems with the production details or the actors. In addition, I had wrangled a last minute booking on the East coast.

This booking was at the historic Ford's Theater in Washington, DC, the site of President Lincoln's assassination in 1865. Before it, I had scheduled in a break of a couple of weeks while the scenery for the show was trucked across country.

I called my trucking company in California, on arrival at the theatre in DC as our stage sets had not arrived.

'Road Hog Trucking. Move it or lose it, what can I do ya for?'

'Ford's Theater in Washington, DC here. Where's my scenery?'

'I don't know, where'd ya leave it?'

Great! My whole financial future was teetering on the brink of failure, and I get the Jerry Lewis of long-haul trucking.

'Look, how can I make this clear to you? You promised me my sets three days ago.'

'Oh yeah, the play people. There was a slight miscommunication here, but we're back on track now. Don't worry about a thing.'

'What kind of miscommunication?'

'Funny story, that. The shipping orders said Washington, so our guy put your stuff on the Pacific coast route.'

'Pacific coast route?' I cried, panic creeping up my spine, 'But we're in Washington, DC! You know, across the country!'

'Yeah, I know that now. Lucky for you we were able to catch our driver just outside of Grant's Pass, Oregon. We got him to trans-ship the whole load onto the eastbound service. We should be there right on time.'

'But right on time was three days ago. There's no more right on time. The most I can hope for now is almost too late!'

'All right lady, calm down. It's not like we're missing a load of fresh salmon or something... like last week. It's only a play. Jeeze!'

There wasn't much to be done, so I had the cast rehearse without a stage set. Two more days went by and still no scenery. Terror set in. If there was no performance, it could wipe out all my profit for the cottage fund to say nothing of breaking my contract with the theatre. The first performance scheduled was a sold-out matinee the following day and the stage set finally arrived only two hours before show time. After it was unloaded, the stagehands barely had a chance to set it up and nail it in place. There was no time left to accommodate the rake, or slope, of the theatre stage, and the one at the ancient Ford's Theater was extreme, causing every piece of scenery to lean forward at a thirty-degree angle.

I had to come up with an idea to save the situation, and the only crazy one I could think of was to have all the actors lean forward at the same angle as the set. We maintained this difficult balancing act until the last scenery change in the show. This change was done in darkness and involved all of the actors on stage. My task was to slide a scenic panel across a backdrop, but because of the set's wild angle it got stuck. Just as the light came up I gave it a violent tug which was too much for the fragile panel and it came away from its moorings with a loud splintering crack. It released with such force that I was sent lurching down the steep slope of the stage towards the audience. Now off balance, I gained speed alarmingly as I headed crazily downhill towards the front row of seats which were filled with elderly matinee ladies. Several tourists chose this moment to photograph the box that Lincoln had occupied, and a barrage of camera flashes blinded me. As I careened towards the elderly ladies down front, broken scenery still in hand, they screamed and fled down the aisles. By the time my sight had cleared, I found myself teetering backwards and forwards, like a tightrope walker, on the very edge of the stage. It seemed an eternity before I finally regained my balance and made as dignified an exit as possible, carrying my jagged piece of scenic panel.

Despite all these disasters, we managed to get through the run of the show with a good profit to add to the cottage fund. Afterwards, I remembered what my mother had always said. 'If something's easy, everybody would be doing it.'

Yes, Mum. I see what you mean.

Five

PAVILIONS OF SPLENDOUR
Filkins, Broughton Poggs, Slad

We arrived back in England the following summer in a cheery mood. We were happy to be renting Stable Cottage again from the Brigadier and his wife and we had money in the coffers from our money-making schemes and a lead to pursue on a cottage.

On the morning following our arrival, we had a leisurely breakfast before setting off for the village of Filkins to continue our search. I couldn't wait to indulge in one of my favourite pastimes, reading the English newspapers. Almost the first thing I saw made me laugh. It told of a woman who managed to capture an escaped parrot one afternoon in her local park. She immediately put an ad in her neighbourhood newspaper, hoping that when the bird was claimed she would get a reward. But her expectation of receiving a nice chunk of money was dashed when she realised, after a day or two, that the owner of the bird probably deliberately released it into the park. She came to this conclusion because the parrot screeched through Tchaikovsky's 1812 Overture, complete with spectacularly loud sound effects of gunshots and exploding cannons, every two hours around the clock. No one responded to the ad.

It was a warm sunny day, and after breakfast we set off to follow up on our lead in the side-by-side villages of Filkins and Broughton Poggs, situated between Lechlade and Burford. Even though the cottage we were seeking was not yet on the market, we wanted to view it from the outside to know if it was worth pursuing.

There are very few street signs in Filkins and Broughton Poggs, so we knew there would be some difficulty finding this property, despite the fact that we had brought along our photo. However, we didn't want to ask for directions as this might alert some of the local villagers to our quest. Many of them would have a waiting list of their own for a cottage perhaps, for friends and relatives.

We parked our car where the Alvescot Road splits off to the east. Nearby were the gates to Broughton Poggs Manor, which was said at one point to have belonged to Anne of Cleves, one of Henry VIII's wives. There must have been pre-nups even in those days because she got the manor as part of her divorce settlement in 1541. We wandered along the manor's driveway, which for part of its length is also a public footpath, and found the beautiful Broughton Poggs Church dedicated to St Peter. It is Norman, with a squat saddleback tower, and is hidden behind farm buildings. It is well worth a look as it has several interesting features including two small Norman doors, a narrow chancel and a tub-shaped font. After exploring the church, we wandered around a little more looking for the cottage, which was proving hard to find.

Suddenly, to our amazement, we came upon an unusual sight in a Cotswold village, an open-air swimming pool. It was surrounded by a grass verge dotted with young families happily munching on picnic food and diving into the water. It looked lovely with its backdrop of ancient cottages. Then I remembered from my Filkins research that this village had the good luck to have been blessed with a sort of sugar daddy. His name was Sir Stafford Cripps, a socialist and Chancellor of the Exchequer in England around the time of the Second World War. He had given Filkins the swimming pool, a bowls club and a whole village centre including hot baths, a health clinic and a children's playground. Everything is still there except the health centre which is now a small post office and village shop adjacent to the pool.

Next, we walked around to Swinford Museum named after 'Old' George Swinford whose son, Young George, has been its trustee for years and years. This museum is open only once a month, so any visits have to be timed carefully. It is well worth the effort, however, as it is full of treasures collected in and around Filkins, including piles of ancient farm implements. 'Old' George lived to be a hundred and, in the museum, it is possible to buy a copy of his book *The Jubilee Boy* which describes the life he lived in the village.

We loved a bit in the book about a war between the small village of Filkins and the nearby hamlet of Little Faringdon that took place in the eleventh century. The war had lasted a day and a half and apparently the only casualty was a donkey. Obviously rivalries go back a long way. In fact, Young George told us that, although Filkins could support quite a good rugby team, unfortunately it must make do with two rather mediocre squads as the Normans still refuse to be on the same side as the Saxon men of the village. Talk about holding a grudge!

Next to the museum is the village lock-up where the local drunks were thrown, in past times, before going in front of a magistrate the following morning. We crowded inside this minute cell and closed the door to get the feel of being imprisoned there. The iron door clanged shut and the cell smelled musty and damp as we got a good look at the gruesome mantrap placed at the back. This gave a hint of the terrible tortures that must have gone on.

By now it was close to lunch time and we asked a local villager for directions to a pub. He sent us on a hike through the lanes to the seventeenth century inn, The Five Alls. Randy was fascinated by this odd name which is explained on the inn sign. Originally, this showed the Queen who governs all, a lawyer who pleads for all, a parson who prays for all, a soldier who fights for all, and a farmer who pays for all. Some time ago a different mixture of Alls were used, the Queen having been replaced by the Devil who takes all.

Bob, the innkeeper, gave us a grand tour of his place when he saw that I was interested in the architecture. One of the rooms, very romantic and quaint, that he let for accommodation, was tucked into the attic, among the eaves, and reached by a twisting, narrow staircase. The floor in the bar had marvellous flagstones and though the inn had gone through many remodels it still retained the cosiness of its origins, which was that of several old cottages having been knocked together.

We ordered lunch while we drank a pint of Brakspear Ale at the bar. It seemed clear that we would never find the cottage we had come to see without some help and so I made inquiries in a roundabout way. Bob told us that the cottage we were after had already changed hands as it had been sold to a member of the owner's family. We were instantly deflated, and couldn't believe our lead had evaporated so quickly. We drowned our sorrows with another beer and ordered lunch, which we had in the pub garden. Our favourite taste treats were the appetisers: a delicious dish of melted goats' cheese and bacon on Portobello mushrooms, in addition to fresh calamari, lightly dusted with a parmesan cheese batter.

As we enjoyed our meal, we overheard a conversation between two old country boys who were sipping their pints of ale at the next table. From their conversation, we figured out that one was named Jim and the other, who had a dog curled up at his feet, was Harry. Another customer, a stranger to the village as it turned out, was having a drink nearby. He glanced over at Harry's dog a number of times and finally he came over to his table.

'That's a fine looking dog you have there.'

'Yes,' said Harry, 'he's a really good mate. He caught two ferrets just this morning. Are you from these parts?'

'No,' said the stranger, 'I'm just passing through, but I've been looking for a dog like that. Would you be willing to part with him?'

'Well, for the right price I might,' came the reply.

These two haggled for a while and made a deal. The dog was led off by his new owner and looked back sadly at Harry as he was driven off. Another acquaintance who had heard this exchange strolled over to Jim and Harry.

'Harry, how could you sell him just like that?' he asked. 'He looked like a damn good dog.'

Jim chimed in as Harry just sat and smiled.

'Harry here's no fool, that's the third time he's sold 'im this year. First opportunity that dog has he comes right back to Harry.' They both laughed and finished off their pints of beer.

As we were paying our bill Bob told us that we mustn't leave Filkins without visiting the Cotswold Woollen Weavers' Barn. So we set off and found it on the way back to the car. As we strolled along, we took photos of the dozens of sheep in the fields. Apparently, great flocks of sheep had roamed the hills in these parts for hundreds of years and their fleece was exported throughout Europe. The medieval wool merchants became rich and built their wool churches all over the area. A wool tax even paid the ransom of King Richard the Lionheart when he was captured during the crusades.

As we entered the Cotswold Woollen Weavers, which is in a huge converted barn, the first thing that struck us was the strong smell of wool oil – tweedy and delicious. Crammed into the ground floor room, and above on the first floor, were several massive antique weaving looms. Weavers were dashing around overseeing their shuttles and it was wonderful to see yards of cloth being woven right there. I loved the loud clanking, whirling and clattering noises the machines made, even though I wanted to stuff my fingers in my ears, and it was fascinating to see how cloth has been woven since medieval times.

Filkins and Broughton Poggs had so much to offer that we left very cast down that our lead on a cottage there had fizzled out. We were now right back to square one in our search and, as soon as we returned, I logged on to the *Prime Location* website and to another called *Pavilions of Splendour* that dealt only in seventeenth century buildings. As I scanned the website, I daydreamed about what it would be like to live in those sixteenth- and seventeenth-century cottages when they were first built. People of those times had to have been hardy souls because there were absolutely no modern amenities. There was no electricity, running water or bathrooms. In many cases there was no window glass, mother-of-pearl shells being used instead. These shells were fixed between narrow stanchions called mullions and couldn't have let in much light. The entire floor of a typical cottage was made of locally quarried three-foot square flagstones. At most, loose straw or a rush rug would be thrown down on top of them. Today these flagstone floors are worn and uneven from three or four hundred years of foot traffic. They have hills, bumps and a wonderful patina. The walls are on their way to being two-feet thick, often made with wattle and daub or stucco. This would have the effect of keeping the home cool in summer and warm in winter. Warm, that is, with a fire in the grate. Without a fire, the damp from the ground would seep up through these porous flagstones because in those days the cottages were built without foundations. If there was no firewood around, it must have been pretty cold in the winter. The Romans introduced central heating to England during their invasion and occupation, but, unbelievably, it hadn't caught on among the British and by medieval times, when the Romans were long gone, it seems to have disappeared altogether. In fact there are still many houses in England without central heating today.

Fortunately, most cottages these days have had modern amenities added. From studying the cottage sales on websites, I realised that there is a lot to know about conservation and the permits needed if any kind of remodelling is to be done. Also, I was beginning to see that the older houses and cottages were described in different grades, which I didn't understand. So I researched the information that explains these listings.

Apparently, English Heritage divides the merits of old buildings into grades. Grade I denotes any building constructed before 1700. Grade II* (note the star) covers important buildings of special interest. Grade II covers buildings of special interest that warrant every effort to preserve them and cannot be demolished or altered without consent or planning permission.

When I got back to the *Prime Location* website I saw that all the cottages with Grade listings were the most desirable and were also the ones that were beyond our means. Feeling very discouraged, I tried to recall some more techniques my mother had used, beyond the caffeine jolt method, to achieve her dream of buying a cottage.

I thought hard about what my mother did when I was a kid. It came back to me how thrifty she was about everyday things. She lived well but beyond that hardly ever indulged in any luxuries, saving every extra penny for her property deals. She had only one property at a time and would roll it over for a new one every few years, waiting until the housing market was just right to make her move, always selling high and buying low. She increased her profit every time and became a mini property tycoon.

I could take a lesson from this in living more economically. My mother could make a banknote stretch until it screamed. I remember a good example when I visited her once in England. We were both trying to watch a Wimbledon tennis match on her television.

'Mum, this picture is so bad, you can't tell whether the ball is in or out – the snow on the screen is the same size as the ball.'

'Really dear? So it is. I suppose I'm used to it.'

'This TV must be twenty years old. Let me buy you a new one.'

'No, save your money. This TV has years of wear in it.'

'But Mum this programme looks like Shackleton's expedition to the Antarctic.'

'It has got a bit worse lately. I've got the receipt somewhere. I think I'll take it back.'

Although she was a whizz at property, she could be quite muddleheaded in other areas and conversations with her were often an adventure in a logic-free universe.

'Why have you changed the colour of your hair, dear?' Mum asked one day when she called from England.

'What?'

'Yes, why have you gone from a blonde to a redhead?'

'But, Mum, I haven't!'

'It doesn't suit you dear – trust me on that.'

'What are you talking about?' I knew that if I hit myself on the head with a shoe I'd have a better chance of following this. 'Mum, you're not making sense.'

'I'm telling you your hair is as red as that Lucille Ball.'

Suddenly it dawned on me. I had made a movie called *Bullshot*, which was now being shown on English television.

'Mum, it's that TV set isn't it?'

'I don't know dear, but promise me you'll dye your hair back to blonde.'

'You've still got it and the colour is on the blink now too.'

'Oh is that it dear? I thought that maybe your producer had gone behind your back and changed your hair colour without telling you.'

'Mum, promise me you'll buy a new TV set.'

'Well, I'll see about that. Tell me something else; are you trying some new make-up, because in the film your face looks really blue?'

Dotty as she was at times, I had to admire her. She got her cottage in Norfolk and it made her very happy.

The next day we had a call from one of the estate agents about a property that was close to our price range. A little more wary now, we wondered what the tragic flaw could be. The description looked fine. A little on the small side – in fact it was minute, but looked very pretty from the picture. It was a fixer-upper; two bedrooms and a bathroom upstairs and a living room and kitchen downstairs.

We were so anxious to see it that we arrived a good ten minutes early for the viewing that had been arranged. The cottage was at least three hundred years old and even lovelier than its photograph, with honeysuckle and roses growing over the front door. I started to fantasise about us living there and having tea parties on the lawn while we played croquet. The cottage was immediately suffused in a romantic haze in my mind, which blotted out some of its flaws. It was empty, so we ooo'd and ahhh'd over the front for a few minutes before climbing over an adjoining wall to get into the field that surrounded the cottage. This we did in spite of a sign that warned us it was private property. Rounding the fence at the end of the garden, we came face to face with a bull. A great big panting bull! The two of us and the bull stopped dead in our tracks. Fortunately the bull was as surprised as we were, his eyes incredibly wide and startled, and it took him a couple of seconds to react. During this brief lull we dashed back around the corner of the fence. We could hear him charging after us. We ran faster than we ever have in our lives, scrambled over the wall and landed in a heap back on the grass.

Trembling from head to foot, we had just finished dusting ourselves down when the estate agent pulled up in her car.

'Oh you're early,' she said, 'I'm so glad you've had the sense not to go in the field to look at the garden. It could've been very dangerous. I forgot to warn you there's a mad bull in there called "Chasin' Mason". You don't want to get anywhere near him!'

Even though we really liked this cottage and were quite willing to have a mad bull at the bottom of the garden, in the end it didn't work out. It had never been updated, it seemed, since the year 1700 and there would have been a lot of work to do to make it comfortable. In the kitchen there was an ancient chipped butler's sink with one rusty tap and the room was so small that an extension would have to be built to house the normal kitchen appliances. In addition, every room seemed to need a major repair of some kind.

I had heard that it is quite difficult to get structural work done on a centuries-old cottage in England. The remodelling permit process is quite tricky and it's very time consuming to push this through the local county council. Sometimes, a permit has to be submitted a number of times before it is accepted. Also, when the remodelling is done, the county council can mandate that only certain original materials be used. These can quickly become ruinously expensive.

Randy and I noodled around with the idea of getting a contractor over to look at the cottage and give us an idea of what it would mean money-wise to remodel. It's always made to look easy on those TV programmes where old houses are fixed up, but the reality is often different. I had visions of the two of us becoming the people we had seen in a *New Yorker* cartoon. This showed a drawing of an old man looking like Methuselah with a long grey beard and his equally ancient wife. They were sitting in front of their unfinished remodel and were telling a friend, 'It should only be another ten years before it's done.'

I tried to peer through my 'romantic haze' and as I did I saw that roof tiles were missing and there were alarming dips in the floor of the bedroom. After a while I realised that I didn't really need to bring a contractor to look at the cottage. Charming as it was, I didn't want to get us involved in this much remodelling.

Here was this cottage's tragic flaw: despite its good location and beautiful 'Squirrel Nutkin' look, it was too big an undertaking to put right. We were disappointed but determined to carry on.

To buck ourselves up we set off early the next morning for a walk that I had wanted to take since reading the charming book *Cider With Rosie*, which was written by one of England's greatest pastoral writers, Laurie Lee. This author is not that well known in the US but in England his books are now required reading in many schools. *Cider With Rosie*, in which Laurie Lee describes his childhood and coming of age, is one of my favourite books and is set where the author was raised, in the village of Slad, just a couple of miles north of Stroud. The Woolpack (Laurie Lee's local pub), the cottage in which he lived as a child and the village school he attended are all situated along the main street, which is little more than a country lane.

The surrounding Slad Valley has such steep terrain that modern farming machinery cannot be used there and all the farming is still done in the traditional manner. This has made the village, set in this isolated valley, feel like the land that time forgot. As we drove through it we glimpsed the incredible views from Swift's Hill, which we were glad to see were included in our walk.

When we reached Slad we naturally stopped first at the Woolpack, a two-storey stone inn dating from the sixteenth century, whose name acknowledges the tremendous wealth generated by the wool merchants through the centuries. Nowadays, however, it is associated mostly with Laurie Lee. His curious readers often visit to see the seat that was always saved by the publican solely for Laurie. This is next to his signed portrait and a pile of his books for sale.

The Woolpack Pub, Slad

While Randy got our drinks, I hunted through this stack for a book that I had been unable to find anywhere else. It was entitled *Two Women* and primarily featured photographs that Laurie Lee had taken of his wife and daughter. This book wasn't included in the pile of books and the publican didn't have a copy of it, but promised to produce it by the time we'd finished our walk.

Several of the locals heard this exchange and as we drank our pint of beer they told us stories about this famous author. One old boy talked about the time, several years earlier, when a school bus came by and stopped right by Laurie Lee, who was sitting outside the Woolpack, basking in the sun. A school kid leaned out of the bus window.

'Does anyone know where Laurie Lee is buried?' he asked.

Laurie replied, 'Well, he's usually buried right here in the pub.'

When he finally died a few years later, he was laid to rest, at his request, in the churchyard opposite. He wanted to be positioned to have a good view of the pub and he got his wish.

We left the old boys laughing over their recollections and set off on our walk. We strolled downhill from the pub until we found a footpath to Slad Brook in the bottom of the valley, then set off for the hillside, passing the Elliot Nature Reserve on the way, and followed the path to Swift's Hill high above us. It was a steep climb with only one place to rest before the top. But, once we got there, what a view! It was a sparklingly sunny day and we immediately forgot the exertion of our climb as we looked around. The steep slopes of the Slad Valley and the rolling hills beyond were dotted with sheep and cattle. In the distance we spotted the tiny hamlet of Elcombe nestled in the hillside, its stone cottages framed by the valley's slopes. We stood on the top of the hill for a long time in the sun and the breeze as we drank in the spectacular views, feeling as though we were on top of the world.

Finally, we descended down Knapp Lane, through Elcombe, past signs to Furness Farm and took a lane that turned sharply to the right. This led us to a track that took us downhill through Redding Wood and into the Slad Valley. The cool dark mustiness of Redding Wood after the bright windy hilltop was a wonderful contrast and we really enjoyed its mysterious, gloomy atmosphere. It was like something from a Tolkien novel. We continued through the trees, downhill past Slad Brook until the track joined Steanbridge Lane and returned us to the Woolpack.

Our walk had taken us on a journey of over two strenuous miles and so we were very hungry for lunch. This was our lucky day – a Sunday actually – because a whole lamb was being barbecued in the pub garden and served for the traditional Sunday lunch, which is always more of a feast in England than any other meal. The scent of the lamb, slathered in garlic and rosemary, wafted up to us from the garden and drove us into a lyrical homage to all sheep everywhere. When it was served it tasted like 'heaven on a stick' – my highest compliment. It came with all the trimmings, including mint sauce, a sage dressing, cauliflower cheese, and, of course, roast potatoes.

After lunch the publican beckoned to us from behind the bar. He smiled and said our book would be arriving soon. A short while later, as we finished our coffee, two women walked into the pub and I was thrilled when the publican introduced us to Laurie Lee's widow Cathy and his daughter Jessy. They had brought Laurie's book *Two Women* with them.

I purchased the book and, after signing it, they sat chatting with us for quite a while. When it was time to leave, Cathy told us exactly where to look for the cottage that Laurie Lee had lived in as a child and after we said goodbye we wandered along the main street until we found it set below the road down an embankment nearby. It was fascinating to see the actual setting of Laurie's book and imagine him living there as a small boy.

Randy and I decided that Slad might be an excellent place to settle if we could find a cottage, but there was not even one estate agent's board in sight and a local told us that the cottages in these parts rarely ever changed hands. When they become available, they are passed on to relatives and friends down through the years.

As we sadly left the beautiful Slad Valley we decided that our visit there had been one of the highlights of the summer. If the reader hasn't already come across *Cider with Rosie*, I highly recommend it.

Back in Stable Cottage we continued going through the viewing suggestions from the estate agents but none were suitable. There were no more leads despite our having put the word out to everybody we knew in several villages. So we took a break from cottage hunting and did some work rehearsing a new play we were writing.

The next day we ran into Mrs Murgatroyd who invited us for a drink that evening at the Manor House. We arrived at the cocktail hour and were greeted and served sherry and smoked salmon sandwiches. Mrs Murgatroyd took me off, almost immediately, to see some new plants she had in the conservatory and we left Randy and the Brigadier chatting together in the drawing room.

We walked into the conservatory and Mrs Murgatroyd insisted I sit down and listen to her. With a steely look in her eye she launched into a diatribe.

'Why do you young gels have this silly notion that there's a perfect man out there? There's not.'

'Wh... What?' I stammered. Mrs Murgatroyd then stood up and acted out her next sentence.

'Men are like rogue elephants in the jungle. Stomping around, waving their trunks in the air and making a lot of fuss about nothing.'

'I'm not sure I unders...' I tried to interject before being cut off.

'With a man, you've got to know when to play out the leash a little and when to pull the choke in tight. Take my husband for example. A while ago he managed to blow up the septic tank. Now that's grounds for divorce right there. But the next chap you marry could leave the sluice gates open by the river and flood the entire village. After that you would wish you still had the husband who blew up the septic tank. Do you see what I mean?'

'No, I don't.'

It seemed that every time we had a conversation with the Brigadier and his wife it ended in a hilarious comedy of errors.

'Well, you will understand what I mean in time,' Mrs Murgatroyd raced on. 'You'll realise that it really is rather lovely to grow old with someone you truly love even if you can't stand them.'

'But I thought you and the Brigadier were happily married.'

'We are. I am absolutely devoted to him.'

My head was beginning to spin. Mrs Murgatroyd continued.

'It's true that he drives me absolutely batty, but with time the love grows underneath, so you see my dear you've got to make yourself hang on.'

'I don't mean to be rude, but what on earth are you talking about?'

'Why you and Randall of course, we've grown very fond of you – you're very good company for drinks and we don't want you to divorce.'

'What? Divorce? Where did you get that idea?'

'I couldn't help overhearing you in your cottage when I was gathering roses yesterday at the bottom of the garden. You were having a ghastly row and talking about divorce.'

'No we weren't...'

'But you were, I wasn't trying to overhear but you were shouting so loudly there's no way I could have mistaken what you said.'

'But I've no intention of divorcing... I...'

Suddenly I had that 'I've just been smacked on the head with a wet trout' realisation.

'Oh my goodness, of course... Randy and I were rehearsing a play!'

'What?'

'Yes, we're writing a play together and we were trying out a new scene where a husband and wife threaten each other with divorce.'

Mrs Murgatroyd chuckled over her mistake, I breathed a sigh of relief at returning to the real world, and shortly afterwards we rejoined the others. Randy was looking a bit cross-eyed and I realised that he must have been getting similar treatment from Brigadier Murgatroyd. Sure enough, later on, he told me how their conversation had gone. The moment they were left alone, the Brigadier started in on Randy.

'You've got to make it work.'

'Make what work?' asked Randy, totally mystified.

'Marriage. I know... men and women are two different species, they just don't go together. But what do you think would happen to a nation without wives? We'd all spend so much time being happy that nothing would ever get done.'

'What?'

'Good God, man, there's only one answer. Have another bloody drink!'

After all the misunderstandings, we had a good laugh together and then asked their advice about house hunting. Mrs Murgatroyd had a brilliant idea. She told us of a service that, for a fee, specialises in finding out about cottages before they are put on the market.

We signed up with one of these services the next day and were immediately set up with a viewing of a cottage in our price range in Kelmscott, the small village that we had seen earlier on our river trip. I had a tingling feeling. It felt like a premonition of something good about to happen.

Six

THE GOOD LIFE - FOODIE STYLE
Chastleton, Southrop, Eastleach

Our appointment to view the cottage in Kelmscott was set for three o'clock in the afternoon. We knew quite a bit about this charming village from our visit by boat when we had toured Kelmscott Manor.

This cottage was being sold privately and the seller's representative was to meet us outside. Arriving early, we found the empty cottage a short way from the church. It was in a terrace of cottages a few yards along a side lane that petered out in a field. The cottage wasn't seventeenth century, as I wanted, but early Victorian. However, it was still very attractive, its big advantage being that it was the last one in a terraced row, divided from the field solely by an ancient hedgerow. Its position meant that it had lovely views on three sides, especially from the upstairs windows. The cottage had potential, but we could see that, as it stood, it needed a lot of tender loving care.

Unlike some of the other cottages we had seen, everything in it was in good working order. The rooms were bare and echoing, but had many original features including oak floorboards, beautiful crown mouldings and window frames in good condition. I had always dreamed of having a working fireplace in the bedroom of my cottage and this one sported a beauty. It was easy to imagine how good the cottage would look after a remodel.

The garden was quite large and rambling and as we strolled around all we could hear were birds singing and the occasional mooing of a cow in the field beyond. The roof was in good shape, none of the windows leaked and all the brickwork seemed fine. Although this cottage needed redecorating, updating and probably some repair, it could be lived in and the work done gradually. Best of all, it was in our price range. We liked everything about it. I started to hum with excitement. Could this be the one? We were told that it was owned by a local farmer who had used it, until recently, to accommodate his farmhands, the last of which had been one of his cowmen. The cottage had been in his family for years, but now the farmer was ready to sell. We guessed that this was probably why he was offering it at a fairly reasonable price. He had no mortgage to pay off and wanted to sell it, perhaps because his farming wasn't paying well at this time.

We knew we had to move quickly as we weren't the only clients using this particular early-bird cottage-finding service. As we walked around the cottage one more time, we discussed if we would be comfortable with buying such a fixer-upper.

Randy could tell that I was gung ho with this concept as I was already choosing colours for the paintwork.

'What do you think of Farrow and Ball's French Grey for the outside trim Randy... or should it be... Smoked Trout?'

'I know why you like Farrow and Ball's colours best,' he replied.

'Why?'

'Because so many of them are named after food.'

'You know, I think you could be right.'

By the end of another walk around we had decided – we wanted it. We had already engaged a solicitor in the event that we would be dealing with a buyer who was not going through an estate agent. Now, trembling with excitement, I listened as Randy called from our mobile phone and authorised our solicitor to make an offer to the farmer for a little above the asking price.

The farmer's representative departed, and we stood there staring at 'our' cottage.

'Now don't get too excited,' warned Randy. 'The offer has to be accepted and we still need to get a loan before it's truly ours.'

But he was too late. I was already buzzing. Surely there could be nothing to stop us owning this beautiful cottage. I wanted to go to buy paint and a brush right away. After we had peeked through the windows a few more times, Randy finally managed to drag me away for a stroll around the village. As we walked, we discussed all the good points about living in Kelmscott.

Gargoyle, St Peters' Church, Winchcombe

'It's on the Thames,' I said.

'It's not far from Kelmscott Manor,' Randy replied.

'Right, we could go there for afternoon tea on Wednesdays.'

'Yeah, and stuff our faces with cream cakes as we loll by the river in the garden.'

'When we live here, let's get a boat!'

'Yes, a little rowing boat with an outboard that we could moor in Lechlade.' As we sauntered along, we really liked the sleepy feel the village had. It was bypassed by major traffic and the only visitors were those who came to the Manor, the Plough Inn, or stopped for a while after mooring their boats. Just down the lane we came upon St George's Church. Now that this was going to be 'our' village, I wanted to explore every inch of it. We walked through the churchyard and passed the tomb of the artist William Morris before finding the heavy church door unlocked.

Once inside we saw that St George's is a cruciform church still showing many of its Norman origins. I had heard that there were some amazing wall paintings inside and we eventually found them in the north chapel. Painted in the year 1280 in red ochre, they show scenes from the Old and New Testaments. Details of them are in a framed display alongside. They were magnificent and looked so fresh that it seemed incredible to us that they were almost eight hundred years old. We particularly admired a stained-glass panel in one of the windows that showed St George slaying a dragon. This is from the year 1430. Like the church in Bibury, St George's is of special interest because it is almost unaltered since the middle of the sixteenth century.

Next we toddled off to the Plough Inn, fifty yards further down the leafy country lane. When we had stopped here previously, on our way to Kelmscott Manor, it had been closed but now we found it open. The Plough is only a few yards from the Thames and parts of it are seventeenth century. The bar has the usual uneven flagstone floors and upstairs there are rooms for bed-and-breakfast accommodation, which have all been recently refurbished.

Randy ordered a split of champagne to celebrate and we sat in the pub's flower-filled garden to toast our good fortune. Although he was more cautious than I, even Randy couldn't see any real problems ahead and so we continued our celebration by having an early dinner.

'What dish would you recommend?' Randy asked the waiter.

'The chef is doing a seafood-tasting menu tonight.'

'Really?'

'Yes, we're calling it Seafood Panache.'

My goodness, what a feast it was. This delicious concoction arrived on a large silver platter overflowing with fresh seafood and, far from having dainty little tasters' menu portions, boasted masses of sautéed calamari, fresh crab in a delicate tomato *coulis*, a fish-egg and *crème fraiche* omelette, *moules* in a garlic, wine sauce, and scallop *wontons* in ginger – all of which completely transported us. To make our happiness complete, when we told the owner, who had come over to ask us if we liked the food, that we had made an offer on a cottage in Kelmscott he presented us with a very good bottle of wine on the house.

We hadn't asked the price of the tasters' menu and at the moment of reckoning we looked fearfully at the total on the bill. We were amazed to see that it was ridiculously low, about a quarter of what we expected. What a meal, and if all went well this would be our 'local'!

As the reader has probably gathered by now, food is important to me and my husband. I think my fascination with it was started by my mother who grew up in such poverty that she rarely ever had enough. She was determined that when she had kids they would eat well and often.

'Come on you kids, breakfast is ready,' she would say. 'Let's go to the seaside afterwards; it's really hot today.'

'Oh, yeah, Mum.'

'Hurry up then or we'll miss the train. Don't forget your swimsuits. Come on, the food's on the table.'

'Aww thanks, Mum,' we said as we tumbled into the dining room.

'Now kids, for breakfast I've made fried eggs in butter, grilled tomatoes, pork sausages, green back bacon, mushrooms and fried bread. You can have toast and marmalade afterwards if you want it. If we leave soon we could get some fish and chips on the way. I don't want you kids to go hungry.'

We would arrive at the station after a vigorous walk.

'I'll get the train tickets and you kids go next door. Here's the money. Get what you like and get me a nice big piece of haddock and double chips.'

We would nosh this down on the platform before the train came. After we boarded and had been chugging along for a while we'd get a little peckish.

'Mum, can we have somefink to eat?'

''Course you can. For the train, I made tomato sandwiches or spam and pickle, and there's potato crisps, oranges and double thick fruit and nut chocolate bars.'

And so it would go on, sandwiches for the beach, sandwiches for the pier, sandwiches for the grass sward above the beach and of course for mid-afternoon there would be a big tray of tea and scones, jam and double Devon cream that we would buy in a seaside café and cart down to the seashore.

Then, just in case we were the least little bit hungry on the walk back to the train station, there would be cockles and whelks, jellied eels and shrimp at a seaside stall. Finally, covered in sand and sleepy, we would climb back on the train and just manage to poke down a couple of bars of brazil-nut chocolate before we conked out.

'How are them kids then?' said Dad when he arrived home after we were asleep in bed.

'I'm gonna take them to the doctor tomorra,' replied Mum.

'What... why, what's wrong wiv 'em?' he asked, somewhat alarmed.

'I dunno... but they're really off their food.'

We kids should have been as fat as bacon pigs, but perhaps because my mother never allowed us to watch television and pushed us out to run around, we didn't become overweight. However, all this did make me into a foodie as my mother was an excellent cook.

Randy and I love to cook, but, while I am quite good in the kitchen, my husband is more like a chef. He unfailingly turns out one tasty meal after another with very little effort. He will come home from working on a movie at the studio and cook because, he says, it relaxes him.

Our friends often laugh at the fact that our holiday photos are more likely to be of food than of friends or destinations. I have wonderful pictures of beef Wellington, *poisson* pie and stuffed guinea fowl that Randy has cooked for some special event. We also have photos of food from practically every country we have ever visited. There are shots of *pâté de foie gras*, *coq au vin* and *œufs à la neige* taken in a French *auberge*; *gazpacho* and *paella* snapped in a Spanish villa; and a coconut curry and freshly caught lobster photographed in a tar-paper-shack café on the beach on the Tahitian island of Morea.

All that can be seen of friends or family are their hands passing around the plates, and I can look at a photo of a fabulous meal and know exactly where and when it was taken and it will instantly evoke the local scenery, the friends we were with at the time and, of course, the delicious taste of the dishes shown.

I was so happy to find that the food in the Cotswolds is really good. English cooking, particularly in restaurants and pubs in this region, has improved markedly over the last several years and, these days, is often on a par with the best of French cuisine. In fact the Cotswolds now has so many local high-quality food sources that there is no need to go elsewhere for top-notch ingredients or cuisine. I remember shopping in Cutler and Bayliss of Lechlade and Tony the butcher presenting us with a superb leg of lamb.

'Is this lamb local?' Randy asked.

Tony pointed down the high street just outside the store window.

'It's from Southrop – two miles that way. Is that local enough for you?'

Being an American, Randy had not encountered some of the cuts of meat that are for sale in an English butcher's shop, and even he balked at cuts like pig's trotters, tripe, offal, calves' liver, bull's brain, kidneys, blood pudding and haggis. But it is so wonderful to be in a real English butcher's shop that I don't mind what is laid out in front of the counter.

One of Randy's favourite dishes is lamb pie and he makes it more or less the same way my mother did. The butcher takes a shoulder of lamb and puts it through the meat grinder. This ground lamb is then sautéed with onions, garlic, mushrooms, celery, tomatoes and plenty of seasoning (like *herbes de Provence*), until it is cooked about halfway through.

Randy will then make puff pastry and roll out enough to line a pie dish. Next, he will make the top covering of pastry and cut it much larger than the dish that will be used. After filling the bottom with the sautéed ingredients he drapes the overlarge pastry covering on top then pulls the excess back in loops, rather like a curtain valance, before he thumbs the top and bottom layers together. Heart shapes and other decorations are made with any left over pastry and stuck all over the top. This is then painted with a whisked egg, put in the oven and cooked for about forty minutes.

When it's done, out of the oven comes the most delicious looking country pie, oozing loops of browned pastry and tasting like something I imagine Mrs Bridges would have cooked in *Upstairs, Downstairs*.

There are more and more organic-food stores opening up in the Cotswolds and even in relatively small towns like Stow-on-the-Wold it is possible to go between the organic food shop, the butcher, three or four excellent delicatessens and a couple of bakeries to get the best, freshest, most sophisticated ingredients for a meal you could ever wish to have.

I have put together wonderful 'deli' meals and picnics with the food sold in these shops. For one picnic I chose slices of York ham cut from the bone, celeriac, French *pâtés de campagne*, pasta salads, sun-roasted tomatoes, olives, sourdough baguettes, fresh shortcake and Cotswold honey. All this obtained without stepping outside of Stow.

As it happened we had to pass through Stow the next day on the way to our solicitor's office. We wanted to get our paperwork set up in the event that our offer was accepted on the cottage we had viewed in Kelmscott.

After this was done we decided to make a day of it in the area. I had long wanted to visit nearby Chastleton House, an exceptional Stuart manor, largely untouched by modern alterations. It is off the beaten tourist track and we had a hard time finding signs to its car park located to the south-east of the house. Once parked we had to take a short hike across a field to get to the entrance.

It was wonderful inside, not the least bit over-polished or touristy. Nothing seemed to have been changed – the house itself, the decorations or the furniture – since it was built in the fifteenth century. It had an almost spooky atmosphere. In this house, more than any other in the Cotswolds, I had a feeling of knowing exactly how it must have felt to live there when it was first inhabited.

We were told an exciting story about Chastleton House, by one of the guides. In 1651 Arthur Jones, a grandson of the original owner and a Royalist, was pursued by Oliver Cromwell's soldiers, but escaped to the house after the Battle of Worcester.

This battle was the last of three English civil wars and was fought in September 1651 between the Roundheads, as Cromwell's Parliamentarian army was known, and the mostly Scottish Royalists who were loyal to Charles II.

The Battle of Worcester was won by the Roundheads who handily beat the Royalists, no doubt due, in part, to the fact that the Royalists' 16,000 soldiers were no match for Cromwell's 28,000 Roundheads.

Despite the hot pursuit by Cromwell's men, Arthur Jones made it safely back to Chastleton House and was hidden in a secret chamber. When Cromwell's soldiers couldn't find him, they elected to stay and continue their search the next day. By chance they retired for the night in a room right next to this same secret chamber, and Jones was saved only when his clever wife managed to drug the soldiers' wine with laudanum, allowing him to make his getaway.

As the house had changed so little since 1651, it was easy to imagine him fleeing, in the early dawn, through the very room in which we were standing – his heart in his mouth, hoping desperately that none of the Roundheads would wake up.

We loved the fact that the house had been lived in, with all its wonderful medieval furniture, until 1992. After its last owner moved out it was handed over to the National Trust.

Next, we wandered through the nearby village of Chastleton, admiring its tall beech trees, sycamores and horse chestnuts. We strolled along a lane called Blue Row and took photographs of its cluster of thatched cottages.

After this we headed off to Stow-in-the-Wold and during the five-mile drive I read up on this town, which is a focal point of the north part of the Cotswolds. This small market town has held two Charter Fairs every year since 1107. They began as sheep and horse fairs but are now largely funfairs although quite a bit of trading still goes on. The town square is almost divided into two sections by St Edward's Hall, a perpendicular-style building with Corinthian pilasters, while the remainder of the town square is lined with seventeenth- and eighteenth-century Cotswold buildings.

We reached Stow in time for a delicious pub lunch at The White Hart Inn. I finally gave in to temptation and ordered a plate of fresh fish and chips while Randy opted for bangers and mash, that hearty British staple, consisting of Cumberland sausages with gravy and mashed potatoes. Real comfort food!

While sipping our ale and waiting to be served, I leafed through an English newspaper and picked out an item to read to Randy. This piece had us both laughing with its description of the predicament of a vicar who had acquired a newfangled implant, operated by remote control, to cure his impotence. This was somehow on the same radio frequency as his neighbour's garage door opener. Every time this neighbour opened the garage door... well, you get the picture! One day the vicar's neighbour had his garage painted and during this its door was opened and closed repeatedly. This particularly embarrassed the vicar who was standing in front of his parishioners, at the time giving his Sunday sermon.

After lunch, we enjoyed ambling around and browsing in the town's antique shops, clothing boutiques and picture galleries. Next, we shopped for food in Maby's delicatessen, the excellent butcher's shop and the organic food store. We finished off with afternoon tea in one of the charming tea shops that dot the town, before setting off for our digs.

The next day we got a call from our solicitor. Our offer had been accepted for the cottage in Kelmscott. I was dazed. We hugged each other with glee. Now we were going to own a Cotswold cottage. Everything immediately moved forward as the solicitor got busy ordering a survey inspection, and suggested we instruct our broker to get our mortgage going. He indicated that buying a house in England could be a very lengthy process and that it was a vastly different procedure from the US system. We wrote a cheque for the solicitor's initial fee and sat down to crunch some numbers. Randy is a whizz at this and quickly figured out that if we were careful we might even have a little left over, when we'd bought the cottage, to fix it up.

We called up the Brigadier and his wife to tell them our good news and they invited us over to celebrate. That evening we were all raising a glass to our good fortune. After the toasts were finished, Mrs Mugatroyd pressed us to buy tickets for the annual charity luncheon in the village, which was held to raise money for various community activities. We forked over the money for the tickets and were saying good night when we smelled burning. Mrs Murgatroyd glared fiercely at her husband.

'Darling, don't tell me it's your slipper again,' she said very sternly.

The Brigadier fumbled around with his slippers that had been tucked behind an armchair. When he pulled them out we were amazed to see smoke curling out of them.

'He's always doing this,' said Mrs Murgatroyd, as she grabbed the slippers out of his hands and shook them until his pipe fell out. She then stamped on one of the slippers and was just in time to stop it from breaking into flames.

'Now look what you've done! You will put your pipe in your slipper!'

'That's so I won't forget where it is,' explained the Brigadier.

'But it's still alight!'

The Brigadier picked up the pipe from the carpet and knocked out the smouldering ash. This caused sparks to shower everywhere and instantly start several small fires.

Kelmscott Manor, Kelmscott

'Quick everybody!' shouted Mrs Murgatroyd, hopping about in a frenzy. We joined her and pretty soon all four of us were stomping around the drawing room, in a crazy hot-coal dance, as we put out the smouldering ash. These two could always be counted on for some kind of cabaret and they certainly didn't disappoint this time. We felt a little guilty about having a laugh at their expense as we realised we had become very fond of them.

Before long we received the surveyor's inspection report on the Kelmscott cottage from our solicitor. We were prepared for a litany of essential repairs and were pleased to see that, while there still was quite a list, nothing seemed to be structurally wrong. There didn't appear to be anything to stop us from moving ahead with the purchase. Over time the plumbing and electrics would have to be renewed and a new damp course put in, but we could live with everything as it was for a while.

It felt great to be so close to our goal and that we could give up cottage hunting, relax and enjoy country life for a while. We lolled around for a day or two and then Mrs Murgatroyd called to remind us to attend her fundraising luncheon the next day.

It was held in a marquee tent in the grounds of one of the manor houses in the village and had a wonderful atmosphere – it was like stepping back into another age. This was somewhat due to the high proportion of 'wrinkleys' in attendance and, although the average age may have been about eighty, the lunch guests were a lively bunch and very smartly turned out. The women were in summer suits, hats and frocks, and the men in blazers with brass buttons and cravats. There was a jolly band playing on the lawn and everybody chattered happily, greeting each other with little shrieks, as they sipped their Pimms drinks and streamed into the marquee. Raffle tickets were being sold everywhere and we were urged by Mrs Murgatroyd to buy a big handful of them. She also introduced us to an elderly actor, with an incredibly plummy voice that projected to the back wall of the tent. He was Mountjoy Montague and was there with his wife Felicity.

'You are actors too, how marvellous!' boomed Montague when he discovered this fact. 'The Brigadier has asked me to put on a Punch-and-Judy show for the kiddies at the village hall,' he continued, 'but I think I'll surprise them and give them a little Lear. I do hope you can come. You can't beat the Bard, can you? Crack cheeks crack and break wind break.'

'Actually I think I'm one of the few actors who doesn't like Shakespeare,' I said.

'What? Ha! For a moment there I thought you said you didn't like Shakespeare,' he said with barely controlled rage.

'That's right, I don't.'

Montague's face turned dark purple as he reacted to my statement.

'Don't like Shakespeare?' he shouted, 'but that's impossible! What about the poetry of Malvolio, the majesty of King Henry?'

'Doesn't do it for me,' I replied.

Suddenly he twisted himself into a wonderfully hammy acting pose and declaimed in full voice.

'S'blood which pricks mine own offending eye. Ne'er broach again true error blessed be.'

People around us began to stare.

'How could you not like that?' he insisted.

'I don't understand what it means,' I wailed.

'Neither do I! What difference does it make? It's Shakespeare damn it! Oh, what's the use?' We heard him muttering as he stomped off towards the bar, leaving us alone with Felicity and a gaggle of her friends.

'You'll be staying for the auction won't you?' she asked.

She had one of those cut-glass English accents with a decibel level that was off the charts. I tried to stuff my fingers in my ears without her noticing.

'Do bid on the piece we've donated – it's really rather lovely – see it over there?'

She pointed to a motley collection of donated items.

'It's on the right. The multi-coloured *capadimonte credenza.*'

Randy and I tried not to let our expressions betray what we thought of this amazingly hideous piece of furniture.

'You're staying in one of the Brigadier's properties aren't you?' She prattled on never waiting for a reply.

'You'll love it here. Not at all far from London is it? And don't you find it peaceful? Well, it was until the Brigadier started renting all of his cottages out to those ghastly Americans...'

She stopped mid-sentence with a confused glance at us.

'I say – you're ghastly Americans aren't you? I forgot.'

Without missing a beat she spotted a friend in the crowd.

'Hello Cynthia, lovely hat.' She turned to her friends and in a half whisper said, 'She wears the same one every year.'

'Hello Daphne,' she called loudly to a rotund lady who was lumbering by several yards away. 'You're looking so well. Have you lost weight?' Lowering her voice she said to her friends, 'My God, she looks like a horse – she's gained fifty pounds. And what an unfortunate fashion choice – the stripes in her outfit make it look as if she's wearing a tent. One that seats thirty-five people. Oh look, there's Richard. Hello Richard.' Turning away she said, 'He's still not married is he? He's well past forty and still a bachelor. I must say it makes one wonder, don't you think?'

Before we could answer she spotted a woman wearing a rather garish dress.

'Goodness, look at Sarah! I hope no Teletubbies were harmed in the making of that frock,' she exclaimed, and then shamelessly continued decimating just about everybody at the luncheon.

Eventually we were all shunted over to our tables and as soon as we were seated the vicar gave a speech. We had to stifle our laughter at his tone. He brayed at us as though we were a bunch of naughty children who had just been caught behind the bicycle sheds doing unspeakable things. Words like 'tuck box', 'midnight bean feast' and 'head boy' crept into his speech which bolstered this impression even more. He finished, to very weak applause, and after the speeches we introduced ourselves to our lunch companions at the table.

The old boy to my right had the most amazing mouthful of crockery. He must have acquired the first set of false teeth ever invented because the clattering noise made when he laughed sounded like a stack of dinner plates being smashed with a hammer.

We felt we were in a time warp because there was constant chatter about long ago events. There were fascinating stories of India, some of these peppered with shouts of, 'Get me another *chota* peg!' and '*quai hai.*'

The Second World War was talked about as if it had been fought yesterday, and we were very amused at one exchange.

'What would you have done if a German airman had been shot out of his aeroplane and parachuted into your garden during a dog fight in the war?' asked one old boy of another.

'I would have gone right up to the fellow,' he replied, 'and said, "Would you care for a drink?"'

We were introduced to another old fellow as visiting Americans and Randy chatted to him in his pronounced mid-western accent. We were, therefore, somewhat startled by his comment a few minutes later.

'Have you ever been to America?' he asked.

During all this, we were served a delicious roasted chicken lunch, with new potatoes in mint and locally grown asparagus.

The money raising started while we were still eating, with an auctioneer who was introduced as Wing Commander Brewster. He was obviously ex-Royal Air Force and he got the bidding going with a loud shout.

'Chocks away chaps! Do I see a bid over there at 9 o'clock? Yes, bung ho. What, five pounds for this *capadimonte credenza*? Surely you jest? Ten pounds over there. Going, going... wait a moment, steady the buffs, the Brigadier is waving his hand for fifteen. Gone! For fifteen pounds.

'Somebody start the bidding on this box of fire logs or there'll be a flap on at HQ. Start off at ten pounds. Yes, ten pounds over there by the bar. Come on chaps, you're sitting on your hands. Twenty pounds, am I bid twenty over there? We'll have to do better than that or we'll be flying through flack. The quicker we drop our eggs and head for home the better. Thirty pounds. Going, going, gone to the lovely lady coming out of the sun at two o'clock.

'Any bids on two tickets for *A Midsummer Night's Dream* performed by the Potter's Crouch Amateurs? ...No? ...What's going on – is there illness in the ranks?'

We liked all the odd items that were auctioned, including an offer by a local man to donate two days of gardening. This offer, written on a piece of paper, was held up by the auctioneer.

'Is the gardener handsome?' yelled one elderly female bidder.

While everybody laughed, another feisty old dear raised her hand.

'What's more to the point, what does he look like with his shirt off?'

Other auction items were a set of peppermills, a box of vegetables, a home-made pudding for six people, a trio of bantam-buff Pekin cross chickens, a cut and blow-dry at a hairdressing salon, a week in somebody's timeshare in Greece, and six bottles of elderflower cordial. The auction came to a noisy, laughter-filled close when a husband and wife began bidding against each other and everybody took sides to egg them on.

When we got back from the fundraiser there was a message from our seller, in reply to our earlier request, telling of the arrangements for us to be let into the Kelmscott cottage the next day so that we could take photographs and some measurements.

The following morning the cottage looked even better than we had remembered, as a new crop of peach-hued roses now rambled over the front of the building. We wandered around the garden, snapping away and fantasising about when it would be ours and how everything would look when it was transformed by the different seasons of the year. We especially liked the idea of being in the cottage during the winter season.

As we measured, we imagined the cottage covered in snow and pictured how cosy the living room would be with a roaring fire in the grate.

Next, foodies that we are, we slipped into an overindulgent gourmet reverie of all the foods we would cook and serve in the cottage, starting with afternoon tea. We like afternoon tea around four o'clock and sometimes have it instead of either lunch or dinner. We would have the full deal, often called 'high tea' and ours would feature cucumber or mustard-and-cress sandwiches and anchovies on toast, followed by toasted tea cakes, scones with thick Devon cream (this has to be so thick it can be cut with a knife), home-made blackberry jam, Victoria sponge cake, Bakewell tart, and fairy cupcakes with marzipan in the middle.

This led us on to talking about how, once settled in the cottage, we would cook dishes from old Victorian recipes. I had a bunch of them saved from my grandmother that had been passed down by her mother. I had been longing to try these dishes, but many of them were too rich and heavy for the California climate. However, they would be wonderful to cook in an English winter.

'I want to cook beef suet pudding, steamed with nutmeg and Worcestershire sauce, jugged hare casseroled in red wine and cloves, puffy Yorkshire pudding made with the juice of roast beef and kedgeree made with salmon and pickled walnuts,' I said, remembering every one.

'What about dessert?' asked Randy.

'Hmm, let's see... I know, spotted dick, sticky toffee pudding, brandied cherries and chestnut soufflé.'

'What about a Christmas meal?'

'Oh yes, roasted goose and I'll serve it in front of a roaring fire by the Christmas tree, with roast potatoes, sweet potatoes, parsnips, Brussels sprouts and pease pudding. For dessert it'll be Duke of Cumberland pudding cooked with suet, apples and nutmeg. Lastly, for a nightcap to warm us when we are ready for bed, how about sack posset?'

'What's that?'

'An old-fashioned eggnog made with milk, nutmeg and Madeira.'

I also wanted to try some recipes I had found in a book, *Toulouse-Lautrec's Table*, by Jean-Bernard Naudin and others. Lautrec had cooked for his friends and served them lavish dishes that would probably be far too rich to cook these days and not the least bit practical. Still, I could imagine quite a few of them being perfect for the often freezing Cotswolds countryside in the winter. Lautrec would serve braised wild boar smothered with whole onions stuffed with pureed garlic or maybe brochettes of oysters with *foie gras* and flambéed lobster with *Armagnac* and *crème fraiche*. One of his recipes that especially appealed to me was *écrevisses* (crayfish) in white wine and tarragon.

Some of his recipes such as oysters simmered in a big slosh of gin, or meat roasted in a cup of pig fat, or a goose stuffed with a calf's foot would just be too rich for me to cook today. Pity really.

As we came out of our foodie fantasy, we began to think about where we would go for our evening meal. We had heard a lot about the Swan Inn in Southrop and as it was nearby we decided dinner there would be the way to go. As our visit to the Cotswolds for this year was nearly over and we were going back to the US in a couple of days, we agreed to make this our last blowout gourmet meal before we returned.

It seemed like it would be a good idea to frame our dinner with a before-and-after walk to work off the calories, so we booked a table for very early in the evening and then planned our hike.

We chose a riverside walk that began at the Victoria pub in Eastleach where we would leave our car. We would then walk to Southrop, have dinner and then stroll back to Eastleach. By eating dinner early we could still get back to our car before dusk, which during August, when we were attempting this, can be as late as 10 pm.

We arrived at the Victoria pub in Eastleach which sits high above the village and is surrounded by old stone cottages, one of which we passed after parking the car. An elderly lady was sitting outside, with her door open behind her, and we struck up a conversation.

'Good evenin', 'ow be youse this afternoon?' she asked.

'Fine, what a great old cottage you have.'

'Me name is Louvain. Would 'ee like to come in for cuppa tea?'

We couldn't resist and we were led into her tiny home. She showed us around with obvious pride. Everything was pin-neat and the cottage was furnished with old pine pieces.

'You have an interesting name,' I said, after we settled down with a cup of tea in our hands. 'I've never heard of anyone being called Louvain.'

The Windrush River near Minster Lovell

'Well, I'll tell 'ee the story of it. Me mother and me father owned this cottage before me and in 1914 me father went to fight in the Great War. Every poor soul in 'is battalion was killed save for seven. My pa was one of them that came 'ome you see. When I were born a year after he came back 'ee named me after the battle. The Battle of Louvain.'

It was sad to think that the dark cloud of war had found its way to this peaceful part of the world. Louvain seemed glad of our company, especially after Randy had cracked a few jokes, and when we moved on she waved us a warm goodbye as if we had been friends for years.

We walked the few yards on to the Victoria pub and took in the view of the cottages grouped beneath it. Next we walked down to the clock tower below. Within a couple of hundred yards we found the footpath we were seeking marked with yellow beside it. It was so peaceful to be by ourselves and away from everything. We strolled along the bank, enjoying the uninterrupted views of the river, meadows, trees, and mallards in flight. At a fingerpost we kept to the right and, after a while, arrived at Coate Farm. We crossed its driveway, climbed a wooden stile and hiked across two fields before walking into Southrop by Pear Tree Cottage. We visited the small village church with its splendid Norman doorway and easily found the Swan Inn opposite the manor house. It's a charming vine-covered Georgian inn with doorways so low that Randy had to duck his head to enter. It was once a pub and is now a pub/restaurant with several rooms, each with two or three tables. Everything about the place told us we were in for a treat. We could see we had made the right choice.

'I'll have the *Prosecco frizzante*,' I said to the barman. This was the house aperitif with white peach juice. Randy had one too and it was just the thing to get us going. Later we were seated in a quiet corner and studied our menus at length for the best choices.

'Are you ready to order?'

'Yes, to begin I'll have the cream of white onion and sage soup.'

'The fish soup for me,' said Randy, 'with *rouille*, gruyere and croutons.'

'For the entrée, I'll have the *bourdin noir* with celeriac puree, sautéed mushrooms and red-wine sauce,' I said, rolling the words around with relish.

'Give me the fillet of bream with *tagliatelle*, roast tomatoes and pesto,' Randy said, making his order sound like music.

It was a hard decision as to who had picked the best entrée. I think Randy won as the bream was so fresh and perfectly cooked that it was hard to beat. We still had a little room left for dessert so I tried the vanilla *bavoirs* with mixed berry compote, and Randy managed the lime parfait with fresh mango and coconut cream. Whew!

We didn't stay for coffee because we wanted to walk back to Eastleach while there was still plenty of light. We returned by a slightly different route, making this a circular walk, that took us back up the other side of the River Leach. Initially we retraced our steps, which took us alongside Pear Tree Cottage again and followed the previous path until it divided. This time we took the right-hand path and crossed the river by a very old stone bridge. Next, we turned left and strolled on for a while until this winding path, with its idyllic views, led us to a narrow country lane. We then headed across the fields to Eastleach and the church of St Michael and St Martin. We admired this lovely Norman church and spent a while there before walking through the churchyard and following the old stone path that led to a clapper bridge and crossed the Leach again. This bridge is a 'must see' in the early spring months, when the display of daffodils on the river banks is an amazing sight. Immediately across the bridge is another church, this one dedicated to St Andrew, which is in the parish of Eastleach. We continued straight on and climbed the hill back to the Victoria pub and our car. We had walked off our highly calorific dinner and arrived just as the last bit of daylight left the skies.

The Victoria pub was now open and looked very inviting, so in we went for a nightcap and a coffee. It's a great pub, not too fixed up, with a bunch of locals and farmers on one side of the central bar, with their dartboard, and a few other types like us on the other. We lingered on there until closing time, talking about how sad we were to be leaving the Cotswolds in the next couple of days. But we brightened up on the drive back, as we talked about our cottage and how we would spend more time there when it was ours.

We returned to the US on a very high note, after making sure that our mortgage negotiations were looking good and that we had completed all the paperwork necessary for the purchase.

Seven

THE COTSWOLD WAY
Haresfield Beacon, Cleeve Hill, Painswick

Back in the US we sent more money to the solicitor as the negotiations proceeded. The mortgage we had applied for was taking longer to arrange than usual because of our being out of the country, but our solicitor said that we should have some news soon. Meanwhile we continued to work and save our pennies and I spent a lot of time leafing through magazines and books looking for decorating ideas and choosing paint colours.

About two months after we arrived back we got a call from our solicitor. His office was not good at paying attention to the time difference between Los Angeles and London so we would get calls at odd hours. This time I was awakened from a deep sleep by the phone ringing at about five o'clock in the morning.

'I'm terribly sorry, but you're gazumped,' said our solicitor.

'What?'

'You're gazumped and the purchase of your cottage is cancelled.'

'No!' I yelled in disbelief.

Randy opened one eye.

'What's going on?' he mumbled, still half asleep.

'We're being gazumped.'

'Not without dinner and a movie first.'

'No, Randy, it's already happened.'

'Did we enjoy it?'

'Hardly, it means we've lost the cottage.'

I turned the speaker phone on as our solicitor explained this strange-sounding word that I vaguely remembered hearing several years ago in England and one that Randy had never come across at all.

'Gazumping means that a home seller agrees upon a sale with a buyer but cancels it after getting a higher offer from someone else.'

'No!' I wailed.

'But that can't be legal,' Randy said indignantly.

'Oh yes, I'm afraid it is in this country,' the solicitor continued. 'Gazumping sometimes happens when a property is put back on the market and continues to be open to offers, even after a sale has been agreed upon.'

'But I thought you said the seller had taken the cottage off the market,' I moaned.

'Well, he had after he agreed to the sale, but then later, apparently, he felt that too much time had gone by and we still hadn't completed the sale. He felt sure that he could get more money for his property so he put it back on the market without informing me.'

We were stunned. We had heard from friends in England that buying a house there could be heartbreaking and now we knew what this meant.

'So do we have any recourse?' asked Randy.

'I'm afraid not.'

'Then all the money we've laid out so far on the inspection survey and your fees is wasted.'

'I'm sorry to inform you that it is. Although it is on its way out gazumping still does happen from time to time. Nowadays, it has become a fairly rare occurrence.'

'This system is crazy,' said Randy, 'you could lose your money over and over again like this.'

'Yes, it needs reform.'

Our solicitor was apologetic but there was nothing to be done. We hadn't even been given the chance to match the new selling price of the cottage. It showed how hot the real estate market was in the Cotswolds despite the downturn everywhere else.

There was a lesson to be learned to prevent another gazumping. We needed to have all our ducks in a row in order to move as quickly as possible. We were already pre-qualified for a loan through our broker, but it seems our paperwork took longer to process than normal. We should have tried to speed up the process as much as possible and stay on top of our solicitor.

The housing market had been going down in England generally, but it seems in the Cotswolds it is almost always on the rise. Over time there has been the occasional levelling out, but in the last thirty years home prices have consistently risen. We didn't find this out until after we had been gazumped, but if we had done our homework properly we would have realised the need for quicker action.

Shortly after hearing from our solicitor we got a call from our mortgage broker, who had not received the news of the gazumping, telling us that we were to be granted our loan. Expecting to hear our joy, he was crushed when we told him what had happened.

It was beginning to feel as if buying a cottage in the Cotswolds was like competing in the Olympics. We would need to go into training and get a lot better at the whole process.

When it had all sunk in I had a severe emotional let down. I was devastated and I cried like a baby. In my mind I had already moved in, painted and decorated and chosen the furniture. After a while I realised that I was feeling more than the loss of this one cottage – after all there would be others for sale. There was a deeper feeling of sadness that probably had to do with the fact that my roots were pulling me back to my homeland with a strength I couldn't ignore.

I have always felt a little schizophrenic about where I really belong as my grandfather was an American. I remember hearing stories about him when I was a child and, as a result, from the age of seven I had always had a really strong desire to travel to the US. This was surprising considering that the story that was most frequently bandied about in my family concerned my grandfather, William Francis White. He was a sailor, working on ships on the transatlantic run between New York and London. On various English shore leaves he had met, courted and married my grandmother. They had a son – my father – known as Bill White. When Bill was only three his mother died so my grandfather put him in the care of relatives and went back to sea. He would regularly send money back for his son's upkeep, but one day the money stopped coming and William Francis White was never heard from again.

When my father was about thirteen years old, he set out to find his father, working as a galley boy on the same transatlantic run as his father. Each time he reached the other side of the Atlantic he put advertisements in the New York Times looking for William Francis White. After his seventh ad, the New York Police answered and said that they, too, were looking for William Francis White and that if he replied would my father please let them know. I often wonder what kind of purple past I have because he was never found and we don't know why the police were looking for him.

I loved living in America just as I thought I would, but lately a feeling had been growing in me of needing to spend some significant time back in England. I wanted to do this even if I didn't return there permanently, so my disappointment about the loss of the cottage in Kelmscott was partly due to the fact that this setback would delay my addressing what had now become a raging case of homesickness.

Once I figured this out, my resolve to go on looking was strengthened though I was still having the occasional good cry. Randy, despite all my blubbing, remained the voice of reason.

'We've come this close and if we keep going we'll score sooner or later,' he said.

'But it feels like we're back to square one,' I replied.

'No, we're not and all we have to do is keep at it. Why don't you make a list of our gains so far?' he suggested.

I did and I saw that first, by staying in the Cotswolds every summer, we certainly knew many more people now than when we had first begun visiting the area. This gave us more chances of hearing about a cottage on the grapevine before it reached the open market. Randy thought this was a very important advantage and I had to agree. Also we now had access to a cottage-finding service that we hadn't known about before. It was expensive but could be the key to our reaching our goal.

This is how we had found the Kelmscott cottage, so we knew it could be effective. It was just tragic that we had been gazumped at the last moment.

In addition, we had not known about the websites *Prime Location* or *Pavilions of Splendour* when we started and these gave us instant access to anything that came on the market.

Lastly, there was more money in our bank account than before, although some of it had now been depleted by surveyor and solicitors' fees. This cheered me up. We were not really back to square one. We had progressed, but now we needed another dose of ingenuity and persistence to get us through. We took a rest for a few days then we picked ourselves up, dusted ourselves down and went right back at it again.

An attack on our problem from every angle was agreed upon. We needed more acting "as if", an all out money-making blitz, and more research and development to improve our buying technique.

The money-making blitz was first on the list. We decided to look at all the money-producing irons we had in the fire and made a commitment to go into high gear on all of them. Randy and I called our theatrical and commercial agents and asked for more auditions even if they were of lower quality. From then on it became Hollyweird.

'Hey, how about this one?' my over-caffeinated agent asked. 'They want a female Elvis impersonator. No lip syncing allowed.'

'Much as I want to work, I don't think my singing is up to par.'

A few days later he called again.

'This one is perfect for you. They're asking for an actress who must look British even though she doesn't have any lines.'

'Eh?'

'This British actress mustn't be afraid of heights because she'll be on stilts.'

'What? That's crazy!'

'Hey, this one's wilder. They want someone to play the Transamerica Building – one speech, seven lines.'

'I've never played a building. I usually play people.'

Next, Randy's agent called with a voice audition for a radio commercial.

'Hey, Randy, you do a Sean Connery impression don't you?'

'Yes.'

'Right, listen to this description: It's a rainy night. You're sitting in front of a roaring fire, sharing a glass of brandy with Sean Connery. They want you to say the lines as if you're talking to him.'

'Let me get this straight,' Randy said. 'You called me because I can do a Sean Connery impression?'

'Right.'

'But they don't want a Sean Connery impression, they want an impression of a guy who talks to Sean Connery?'

'I knew you'd understand.'

'So, while I'm in front of a roaring fire with my brandy on this rainy night, what am I doing with Sean Connery?'

'Selling him a vacuum cleaner.'

'I see. What time?'

That was almost as ridiculous as the play I once read that gave the stage direction 'enter the stage as if you have a brother in Canada'.

Later that week, my agent tried again.

'OK then, how about this? They want a female Caucasian kung fu dermatologist who combines martial arts with dermatology.'

'Kung fu, no can do.'

'Well then, try this: an anorexic feminist separatist pig farmer with a keen political awareness and an earthy sexuality.'

'Not skinny enough.'

Not too long afterwards, he called again.

'Can you swim?' he asked.

'Yes.'

'OK, I've got a commercial audition for you at four o'clock – take your swimsuit.'

When I got to the studio, a casting assistant showed me to a swimming pool.

'Here, take this,' he barked, as he shoved a large bar of soap into my hands – this being the product to be advertised.

'The casting director is at the bottom of the pool, dive down and smile when you see her.'

I did as he said and located the casting director, who was at the bottom of the pool wearing scuba gear. I swam by her, held up my bar of soap, and smiled. However, she seemed to be having trouble with her scuba equipment and was too busy drowning to take any notice. I got water in my ears, my peroxided, highlighted hair turned green from the chlorine in the pool and I still didn't get the job.

The next month, my agent sent me on a national commercial audition. This was more like it. These commercials, if they run a good long time, enable actors to rake in terrific money. When I arrived I noticed that the casting assistant was calling the actresses in to audition in pairs. This doesn't usually happen.

I was teamed up with another actress and, when it was our turn, my companion was handed the front part of a horse's costume as I was handed the back end.

'Put your costumes on – join up and gallop around the room,' said the casting assistant. I couldn't believe I was actually auditioning for the part of a horse's ass! When I got out of the costume, I turned to the casting assistant.

'Hey, does my ass look big in this ass?' I asked.

It must have done, because I didn't get this part either. Well, there's no biz like showbiz!

While I was waiting for a decent part to show up, I dug up a screenplay that I had abandoned a while earlier due to writer's block. I figured I could make a great contribution to the cottage fund if I could sell it. I scribed away and finished it in record time, then put the word out that I had a script for sale. Nobody seemed to be buying right then. I had almost given up hope, when I got a call from my buddy Jane.

'I'm having a dinner party and maybe a dip in the Jacuzzi after. Why don't you come and I'll hook you up with a big-deal producer. He could green-light your movie if he likes it.'

I was over the moon – if I could sell a movie script for decent money my troubles would be over.

On the day of the dinner party, I subsequently discovered, Jane was suddenly called away on urgent business and had left her husband John to shop and get everything ready for her to cook when she returned. John, never too smart at the best of times, on this day seemed to be one apple short of a picnic. He shopped at the last moment and got back only five minutes before Jane, who, having been seriously delayed, came breathlessly running in at the same time as the first guest.

'Quick, John!' she said. 'Where are the game hens? They've got to go into the oven right away!'

'They didn't have any – but it's OK, look what I got instead,' he replied, as he lead her into the pantry and indicated a turkey the size of a three year old.

'Oh no,' she wailed, 'that's too big to cook in time.' When she tried to pick up the turkey her wails grew even louder.

'It's frozen!'

'Is that a problem?' he asked.

At that moment more guests piled into the kitchen and Jane was swept up in greeting them. John, meanwhile, grabbed the turkey.

'I'll fix it,' he said.

I had just arrived and was surprised to hear a chainsaw being operated in the garage. John was cutting the frozen turkey up into small pieces in order to make it cook more quickly. I suggested sending out for pizza but Jane wanted to impress the producer and director types, who were now streaming through the door, with her *haute cuisine*. She proposed giving everybody lots of drinks and pretzels while she cooked the turkey in its current form which was small, frozen cubes.

'Dinner will be a little late,' she said with her most sincere fake grin.

In between attempting a miracle in the kitchen and keeping the drinks flowing, she tried but failed to introduce me to the big-deal producer who was caught up with too many other people. Finally, at about ten o'clock, with everyone well tanked up on drinks, the meal was served. However, nobody could eat the small cubes of turkey, served on rice, that were charred black on the outside and raw inside. With dinner a bust, Jane hurried everybody out to the Jacuzzi which by now was overheated.

Most of the guests, including my producer, piled in and splashed around. I sat on the edge, with my soda water, and finally got introduced to him, but before I could pitch my screenplay he excused himself and climbed out of the hot water. He walked unsteadily towards the house but had only taken a few steps before he suddenly keeled over on the grass, dropping like a stone. Some of the women guests screamed and a clutch of people rushed to help him. However, several of these would-be rescuers didn't make it either as they, too, keeled over. I couldn't believe it. People were dropping like flies. It looked like the train platform scene from *Gone with the Wind*. Too many drinks combined with the hot water had done its worst. Paramedics were called but by the time they arrived everybody had come out of their faint. When my producer recovered he was furious.

'What are you people trying to do, kill me? This Jacuzzi was too hot.'

I tried to put a positive spin on things.

'I kinda like it when that happens – a sort of out-of-body experience – it's wild.'

He headed for the door with me trailing after him vainly offering my business card.

'And that awful food!' he thundered.

'You didn't like it?' I said incredulously, 'but that was the best New Orleans style blackened turkey-sushi *étouffé* I've ever had.'

Needless to say the screenplay sale did not work out but Randy was doing much better and had landed a job on a spoof comedy movie entitled *Silence of the Hams* in which he performed the voices of George Bush and Bill Clinton. This added considerably to the cottage fund, but left me a little cast down as my efforts had been so unfruitful. To buck myself up I got out all my pictures of the Cotswolds and went through them. Then inspiration struck. Maybe I could write a travel article based on a highlight of one of my trips, sell it to a newspaper or a magazine and earn some money that way. I did some research and found I needed to write about 850 words for a newspaper's travel section article. Hey, I was a writer and I sure knew my subject.

I went through my journals to find something I had done in the Cotswolds that really transported me. It wasn't long before I came across an entry about a walk Randy and I had taken the previous summer. It was so spectacular and my memory of it so vivid that I looked no further. It certainly was one of the highlights of our visit – a hike to the Haresfield Beacon which took in part of the Cotswold Way.

An article on the Cotswold Way walk would be marketable because more and more hikers were taking on the challenge of completing its 104-mile length and it was becoming the 'in' thing among them to do so. I wrote this experience up as an article and sent it off to the travel section of several newspapers.

The Cotswold Way is a series of linked long-distance footpaths that follow the scarp of the Cotswold Edge. This walk offers magnificent views starting in the south with the Severn Estuary and Severn bridges, continuing onto the River Severn above Sharpness, the Forest of Dean, the Welsh hills of Monmouthshire and the Black Mountains on the Welsh border to the west. May Hill and the Malvern Hills are seen for most of the route, and Gloucester Cathedral can also be viewed along the way.

Further north on the path, above Cheltenham, there are quarries with famous rock features such as the Devil's Chimney at Leckhampton. After Cleeve Hill the escarpment turns to the east, giving amazing views across the Vale of Evesham. The broad expanse of common land known as Cleeve Common climbs upwards from the Winchcombe side to West Down, which is the Cotswolds' highest point. There is a vast array of wildlife to observe here and the Cheltenham side offers spectacular views to the Malverns, May Hill and the far distant mountains of Wales. The villages of Stanton and Stanway are also on this route, as is Broadway.

A ramblers' association first came up with the idea of putting together the Cotswold Way from existing footpaths and the Gloucestershire County Council designated it as a route after that.

To get to the Haresfield Beacon, which is just west of Painswick, requires a drive to the northern part of the Cotswolds. I was interested to discover that there are many ancient hill-top beacon sites in various parts of England. In past times, bonfires were lit on the top of these hills to signal messages, such as the approach of a marauding army, and this practice is said to have gone back to the Iron Age. The Haresfield Beacon was used by Cromwell's men in the English Civil War to signal the approach of his enemies.

We set off to find this beacon quite early one day and along the way noticed how the honey-coloured stone of the southern Cotswold cottages gradually gives way to a creamy grey-and-white-coloured stone the further north we travelled. The result is quite a different look to the architecture.

We made such good time that we decided to stop off in Painswick for a coffee and to explore a little. This charming town, which is on a high spur between two valleys, is an interesting place to visit. The dyeing of cloth became a speciality here in the seventeenth century because the spring water in the surrounding valleys was so pure. The affluence generated from this work must have contributed to the prosperity of the town, as shown by the rows of unspoilt, elegant townhouses built in Painswick at this time.

Painswick's church, parts of which are fifteenth century, is much valued for its colonnade of clipped yew trees, which were planted in the churchyard in 1792. Their sculptural shapes looked like giant lollipops and were a striking contrast to the hard-edged lines of the church spire rising behind them.

We stopped at the tourist information centre to inquire about the six-acre Painswick Rococo Garden that I had heard about. Work had been done to restore it to its original form, which is shown in an eighteenth century painting by Thomas Robins. It's half a mile north of Painswick, and we made a note to visit it at a future date. We found Painswick to be quite different from other Cotswolds towns and put it on our list for more exploration in the future.

Next, we drove on to our pub lunch destination near Haresfield Beacon, the Edgemoor Inn. As our car climbed higher and higher towards the inn, our stomachs rumbled. This was due to having deliberately missed breakfast, so that we could do our carbohydrate loading just before the strenuous uphill walk to come.

Arriving at the inn, we were seated on the terrace and were stunned by the magnificent views of a big valley before us and the whole of Painswick in the distance. This inn is directly on the Cotswold Way and is just over 49 miles from its start. The Edgemoor is known for its home-made food and a couple of hearty steak and kidney pies were just the ticket right then. We ordered a pint each of local Uley Old Spot. This terrific beer was from an independent brewery located a short distance along the Cotswold Way.

We finished lunch and found the view so interesting and the weather so perfectly sunny and moderate that it was a big temptation to bag the hike and just continue the boozy lunch. However, the prospect of even better views up the trail finally motivated us to get going.

Across the road from the inn we followed the signs to Haresfield Beacon, which is National Trust property, and crossed an old quarry before walking through Halliday's Wood. We climbed steadily uphill, puffing and panting a bit on the way, and passed the Cromwell Monument Stone. The hollows in this stone are said to have been used by members of Cromwell's army in 1644 for casting shot.

We saw lots of bumps in the terrain, some of which were disused quarries while others are archaeological remains such as an Iron Age hill fort or a Neolithic chambered long barrow in nearby Randwick Wood. Next, we walked on to Ringhill Farm and from there we reached the beacon. This was on the south-west facing spur of the scarp and we were absolutely knocked out by the view. Or views, I should say, as we were on the highest point of land as far as the eye could see and had an unobstructed 360-degree vantage point. It was truly spectacular. The whole Severn Vale was laid out beneath us and, beyond that, Wales. I now understood why hikers raved about the Cotswold Way. We were glad we had brought our binoculars as we met a couple of helpful hikers who pointed out many landmarks. There was so much to see that we stayed for a good hour before walking along the opposite edge of the hill and reaching Standish Woods.

Descending through the wood, we finally emerged opposite the Edgemoor Inn car park and our vehicle. The walk had been six miles, with most of it on the Cotswold Way. We now felt it would be good to walk the entire length of it, over time, and this had been a great hike to start us off. Although we'd had a good workout, we were so exhilarated by the unbelievable views that we felt ready for anything.

Before I started this article, I had felt down in the dumps from being gazumped, but writing it had been like a trip back to the Cotswolds and now my mood had lifted.

I had finally come around to Randy's point of view – we had come close to getting our cottage and now the question was could we hang on until we finally got there?

Eight

A SILVER LINING
Charlbury, Finstock, Cirencester

'Yabba dabba do!' yelled Randy doing his best Fred Flintstone.

'Yes, that's good,' said the director, 'can you do Barney too?'

'Sure!' said Randy doing an exact sound-alike, 'Hey Fred, let's tell the girls we're going bowling.'

'And what about you?'

I moved over to the microphone.

'Can you give me a Betty Rubble?'

'Barney, we'd better go home, Bam Bam needs his supper,' I said in Betty's American-accented voice.

'Great! OK. Thank you both for coming in. We'll let you know.'

A few months had passed and Randy and I were now auditioning for a cable show in England. It was for a retro channel that was recycling old cartoons and we were trying out for the promotional spots that were needed between the programmes.

After our gazumping in America, it had become increasingly obvious that, unless we were actually in England and ready to pounce on any cottages that might come up for sale, this thing wasn't going to happen. This had been brought home to me after I had spotted two more suitable cottages, but lost them because our offers were too late.

I also belatedly discovered that the seller of the Kelmscott cottage had put a board up outside, advertising it for sale, after he had made an agreement to sell to us. If we had been staying in the area we would have seen this and probably saved a considerable amount of money on a survey inspection and solicitor's fees.

At about the same time that Randy and I were mulling over this realisation, the union contracts for actors and writers ended. Negotiations with the studios broke down and an industry strike was called. We were union members, so now we had no possibility of working. True, we still had some re-run money from all the shows we had worked on in the past but that was it.

I was so cast down I was willing to risk another week of insomnia and succumbed to the lure of more industrial strength tea. The buzz was so strong I nearly levitated. This time the inspiration was instantaneous and I rushed to find Randy.

'I've got it,' I said, 'let's rent our house in Los Angeles and stay in England until we find a cottage.'

'What an idea,' replied Randy doubtfully.

'We can't work and this strike looks like it's going to be a long one.'

'But we've got to find a way to get some money coming in. The re-run money alone won't keep the wolf from the door.'

'I know, but we could look for work in England.'

'I don't know; this doesn't sound like a good idea.'

'But why? We'll be in the same position here.'

'But, where will we live?'

'We'll find a guest cottage in the countryside.'

'Like where?'

'Maybe the Brigadier can help.'

'Well, I suppose it could work.'

'I know it could... maybe this strike has a silver lining.'

The Brigadier had several holiday rents and some longer term ones in various converted stables and barns on his property, in addition to Stable Cottage where we normally stayed. We called on the speaker phone about a longer term rental the next day. The Brigadier answered.

'Hello.'

'Hello,' I said, 'this is the Montgomerys calling from Los Angeles.'

'Who's calling?' said the Brigadier.

'The Montgomerys,' I said twice as loudly.

'You'll have to speak up I can't hear you,' he replied.

'THE MONTGOMERYS!' yelled Randy.

'Are you shouting?'

'YES!'

'It's no good shouting; I'm completely deaf, you'll have to speak to my wife. Wait a moment, I'll put her on.'

'Who's calling?' asked Mrs Murgatroyd.

'It's the Montgomerys from Los Angeles.'

'Hello, are you calling my husband? Because if you are you should know he always uses his bad ear on the phone so he can't hear a thing.'

'Yes, so we gathered. That's why we'd just as soon talk to you,' I said.

'Oh, you want to talk to me?'

'Yes.'

'Well, then why didn't you call me?'

'We did.'

'No, you called my husband.'

'Well, he picked up the phone.'

'You have to make sure I will pick up the phone.'

'How will we know if it's going to be you?'

'Well, you'll recognise my voice. It's me speaking now and, besides, my husband never picks up the phone.'

'Well, he did just now.'

'Did he?' She then called down the phone to the Brigadier. 'Darling, are you upstairs on the extension?'

Next, we heard the Brigadier's voice in the background.

'No, I'm right behind you.'

'Oh,' said Mrs Murgatroyd with surprise, 'how did you get there so quickly? I thought you were on the extension upstairs.'

'Well, I wasn't,' he replied, 'I haven't been upstairs all day.'

'Oh, did you know the Montgomerys are on the line?' she continued to her husband.

'No, what do they want?' he said in the background.

'I don't know, why don't you ask them?' said Mrs Murgatroyd.

'Jolly good idea,' he replied.

'Hold the line, my husband wants to talk to you.'

'No,' I said, 'he can't hear us.' But it was too late.

'Hello, Brigadier Murgatroyd here.'

'PLEASE PUT YOUR WIFE BACK ON THE PHONE!'
I yelled.

'You'll have to speak up I can't hear you.'

'PLEASE PUT...'

'I can't hear anything,' he interrupted, 'they must have hung up.' (CLICK, dial tone.)

After several more attempts we finally got our message through and worked out an arrangement to stay in a tiny apartment in one of the Brigadier's converted outbuildings for an amount far lower than we had paid at Stable Cottage.

We rented out our house in Los Angeles and happily resettled in our new digs in England. Within days of arriving we had travelled up to London for the Flintstones voice audition. Afterwards we made our way back to the Cotswolds from London by catching a train from Paddington station, and as the train pulled out I sat looking out of the windows in a pleasant state of shock. Everything had happened so quickly that I couldn't quite believe I was now in England again for the foreseeable future.

Our plan was to find whatever work we could and in every other spare minute go full steam ahead on the cottage hunt. We'd made a good start by setting up a bunch of job interviews shortly after arriving. Now we were on our way to a cottage-hunt seminar being held by our friends Sandra and Jim who divided their time between their London apartment and their home in the Cotswolds. They knew we had envied their cottage and as we were so disappointed that our purchase had fallen through they decided to take us in hand.

As the train rattled along I leafed through the newspapers I'd bought on the platform. It didn't take long to pick out a couple of items for Randy's amusement. The first was a story of a man rowing the entire length of the Thames for charity, who got caught up with the boats competing in the Henley Regatta and somehow won a race. Randy didn't find the story amusing until I showed him the picture that went with the article. The winner was actually crossing the finish line in an over-sized dog bowl.

Newborn lamb in the Evenlode Valley

The second was a story of two families, each with two children, who lived next door to each other. In their typically reserved English fashion, they had not exchanged a word during their five years of being neighbours, beyond a polite 'Good morning'. Both families were surprised, therefore, to find themselves on the same plane taking them off to their resort holiday. They all ended up in the same 3,000-bed hotel in adjoining rooms. As if that wasn't enough of a coincidence, they discovered they had brought the same holiday reading material – Joanna Trollope's book *The Best of Friends*. It could have been a nightmare, but they got on well together and would sit and chat on their balcony after all their kids had gone to bed. They became great friends and plan to take their vacations together for the foreseeable future. It was not clear, however, whether or not they would speak to each other during the intervening year.

We arrived at Charlbury station an hour and a half after finishing our audition and picked up our car from the station car park where we had left it that morning. Tiny Charlbury Station is straight out of an old English movie, an Ealing comedy, perhaps, like my mother's favourite, *The Titfield Thunderbolt.* The waiting rooms are of wooden construction and quaintly Victorian in style. There are neat rows of flowers and a lily pond, no less, beside the single-track platform. When we alighted, a milling crowd of passengers were waiting to board, all of whom seemed to know each other. Charlbury is in the Evenlode Valley with stunning views across miles of Cotswold hills and the 600-acre Cornbury Park estate. Charlbury, which is six miles north of Witney, is in Oxfordshire and began as a small village in a clearing of the Wychwood Forest. These gorgeous woodlands still largely surround it and the whole area is well worth a visit featuring many interesting old buildings, shops and country inns.

We really enjoy the hikes in this area especially along the bridleways near a wonderful mansion at Ditchley Park. There is also a circular walk that includes the pretty village of Finstock which is part of Cornbury Park.

Finstock features a very fine gabled manor house, and a Gothic Revival church with an elaborate south window by the architect P. Morley Horder. This village's origins are thought to go back over a thousand years as a settlement on this spot is mentioned in the *Domesday Book.*

Every year Cornbury Park throws a wonderful, family friendly bash – a music festival that calls itself a country fayre – but is really a very enjoyable, well organized, low-key rave.

I always really like the drive from Charlbury station to Burford, our destination. It is particularly calming after a nerve-jangling day in London, as the route meanders through the rolling hills of the Cotswolds revealing halcyon views for miles around. It is especially lovely at dusk, which was just now stealing across the sky, and by the time we reached Burford I had relaxed into my usual state of Cotswold bliss.

We drove through Burford and on to our friends Sandra and Jims' cottage nearby. They had promised to help us with our problem by offering some useful tips. The idea was to have our cottage-finding seminar and then later more friends would join us for dinner.

We arrived at their deliciously cosy Victorian cottage and were greeted with hugs, glasses of wine and the aroma of roast lamb wafting from the kitchen. The evening had become quite chilly and a traditional English roast dinner seemed just right.

Sandra and Jims' cottage had taken them two years to find, even though they lived in England and knew all the angles. After a few sips of wine, we outlined our previous efforts and asked where we had gone wrong.

'Nowhere,' said Jim, 'you just haven't cast your net wide enough. The key to all this is to follow up on every avenue, absolutely relentlessly.'

'Where do we begin?' I asked.

'You should make up a flyer saying that you want to buy, and put it through the door of every cottage you fancy,' said Sandra.

'Go out to as many fêtes, barbecues, fund raisers and public functions as you can, near where you want to live, and ask total strangers if they know of anywhere for sale,' said Jim.

'Really? Total strangers?' I asked.

'Oh yes,' he said, 'you have to be assertive, ask everyone you meet, especially people who deal with the public all the time, such as the local hairdresser, the librarian and shopkeepers. These people hear things from all their customers.'

I pulled out a pad and paper and started taking notes.

'Oh, the milkman is a good one to ask,' said Jim.

'And the postman,' added Sandra.

'Yes, and go to as many pubs as possible and just hang around all evening listening to local gossip.'

'No problem there,' said Randy with a laugh.

'If the locals see you around a lot and get to know you, they'll open up more about what's going on in the cottage market.'

'Yes,' added Jim, 'especially if you buy them a drink.'

'And don't forget to get the *Sunday Times* – look in there every weekend as well,' said Sandra.

'Yes, and the Wilts Wuus,' said Jim.

'What's that?'

'*The Wiltshire and Worcestershire Times.* Three or four local papers like this cover the entire Cotswolds. Put an advertisement in them under houses wanted.'

'Get that monthly magazine *Cotswold Life.* They have cottages for sale.'

'Put a sign up too in all the shops that have notice boards.'

'Get involved in community village activities. Join the book club or the coffee mornings. Or volunteer for things. Offer to help organise the garden tour. All the villages have them in the summer. Or help out at a fund-raising fête. You could even start an amateur dramatic society.'

'The whole idea is to get hooked up with villagers and get them to chat to you.'

'Yes, that's good. And don't forget antique fairs,' said Jim, 'there are lots of people at those. There's an antique fair in the Corn Hall in Cirencester every Friday.'

'Yes, and an open-air one in Oxford every Thursday morning – it's near the bus station.'

'Drive around a lot – sometimes you see a sign up where the home owner is selling privately. It does happen.'

'When you are driving around, stop if you see any cottages being remodelled and ask the builders for the owner's telephone number. They might be wanting to sell when it's finished.'

'Go to all the farmers' markets, chat to people and have a flyer handy with all your information on it to give to them.'

'How many estate agents are you registered with?' asked Jim.

'Five or six.'

'Not nearly enough,' said Sandra, 'get a list of them all and go around and register.'

'But that doesn't mean much,' added Jim, 'you have to call each agent once or twice a week and remind them to look for you. They have so many people on their books you have to be a "squeaky wheel".'

'Yes, you need to develop a phone list that you keep adding to every day. Also, even if you find a cottage that you like and start negotiating, don't stop looking. That won't give you so much heartache if it falls through. There, got enough?'

'Whew,' said Randy.

'Many thanks. Wow, this really is a full-time job,' I agreed.

'Well, I'm sure you'll find a cottage before you have to do everything we suggested, but it's good to have all that info just in case,' said Sandra.

'Even if we do find a cottage, I don't know how it's all going to work,' I said doubtfully. 'It seems as if it will be very difficult keeping two homes going if we want to go back and forth between the Cotswolds and Los Angeles.'

'Nonsense,' replied Sandra, 'when you are back in America you do short-term corporate lets. I'll fix you up with an agency that we use.'

I looked around at their sitting room with its beamed ceiling, foot-thick walls and a fire glowing in the copper-clad hearth, and took a deep breath.

'Right! We start tomorrow,' I said, 'and thanks to you I know we'll make it.'

Just then our other actor friends arrived; Rita, who had come down from London, and Michael from his home in a nearby village. I put my notes aside and, after another glass of wine, we all tucked into Sandra's very appetising roast dinner, hot from her AGA. So many good cooks have these stoves and their food seems twice as tasty.

Sandra served a leg of lamb smothered in fresh rosemary and garlic, accompanied by Yorkshire pudding. She had remembered that I am addicted to Yorkshires. Her puddings were very puffy and light as air. In addition, there were roasted potatoes, roasted red onion, parsnips, runner beans, mint sauce made from mint from the garden, rice vinegar and Cotswold honey. This course was followed by Peach Melba with Cotswold ice cream.

After dinner we settled in the living room with our coffee and, as often happens when a bunch of actors get together, tried to outdo each other with theatrical disaster stories from various shows in which we had performed. Randy told of when he had performed once as Lord Hastings in Shakespeare's *Richard III*. The character of Lord Hastings is executed and later in the play his severed head is brought before the other characters on stage as proof of his demise. In this production, Hastings' head had been modelled in *papier mâché* around a football, and it looked very realistic. However, during one of the most solemn moments in the scene, the actor who was carrying this head dropped it. It bounced as if it was in play on a football field. First, one actor leaped to catch it, but it ricocheted in an unexpected direction so another actor went for it. But he too missed catching it as it zoomed off a scenery wall. The whole play fell apart, while every actor on stage had a try at catching the head as the audience dissolved into laughter. Randy said that if his character hadn't been dead already, the humiliation would have killed him.

Michael's disaster story was a winner too. It had happened on tour with Sheridan's *School for Scandal* in Canada. The company of English actors performing it had been so delayed in reaching the first stop, an arts centre, that there was no time to rehearse. This arts centre had three different performance spaces, all of them in use that night and all sharing an actors' lounge linking the backstage areas.

Michael, in his make-up and costume which featured a velvet coat, knee breeches, lace cuffs, and an enormous, powdered, curly wig, hurriedly made his way to the stage for his entrance. However, after leaving the lounge he lost his way and, ran around in desperation before entering a door and finding himself on the wrong stage in front of the audience of another play in the arts centre.

This was a modern-day, angst-ridden, gay drama and the two actors performing it were on stage, lying in bed together, deeply involved in a love scene and apparently naked under the covers. They froze in shocked astonishment as Michael, fearing that he was late for his cue, flung himself wildly on stage in full Restoration costume, curly wig askew, waving a lace handkerchief and loudly declaiming his lines. There was a loud rustling of programmes from the startled audience as they tried to find mention of a third actor in this two-hander. Michael, horror-struck upon realising his mistake, stopped mid-sentence and with a deep bow slowly backed up and exited, flourishing his lace handkerchief in apology.

Meanwhile his own play had almost ground to a halt without him. The actors on this stage were awkwardly improvising lines Sheridan would never have written, as Michael, now frantic to find his play, ran around backstage, screaming loudly enough for the audience to hear, 'Which is the (bleep)ing right door?'

We ended the evening with gales of laughter and many words of encouragement from our friends to continue our quest. All the new information we had gathered certainly made us feel very positive about doing just that. The next day we followed our friends' suggestion and took off to Cirencester to mix and mingle with our newly made flyers. Cirencester, once second only to London in size was then a Roman settlement called *Corinium Dobunnorum* and featured a forum, numerous temples and a basilica. Nowadays little remains of the Roman origins of the town with the exception of a few sections of ruined walls and an amphitheatre now covered in grass. Many Roman artefacts, such as mosaics and religious icons, however, are housed in the Corinium Museum.

Cirencester is noted for its fine market square, which hosts markets on Mondays and Fridays of every week. This town's prosperity is derived from its medieval wool trade and is exemplified by the cathedral-sized church of St John the Baptist. The church's 50-metre tower soars high above the market square and can be seen from miles around. We gave out flyers to a dozen or so friendly folks that we met while exploring the town and left several more of them in an estate agent's office. It felt good to be taking some action but we knew we had a long way to go.

Nine

SO NEAR YET SO FAR
Buscot, Mickleton, Lechlade

'Come over for drinks, around 6.30.'

We had followed up on many of the suggestions made by our friends over the following few weeks, and our invitation to drinks had come from the owners of a cottage who had responded to a flyer put through their door by us about ten days earlier.

We'd had a number of responses from our flyers, and had looked at a good dozen other cottages, none of which had been suitable. Either they required too much work or were very overpriced for what was being offered.

Randy was reaching cottage-viewing fatigue, so I crossed my fingers as we set off to for our 6.30 meeting. We had put out so many flyers that it was impossible to remember exactly which cottage we were heading for as we drove to a small village in the southern part of the Cotswolds. But I suddenly remembered this particular cottage as soon as we reached the outskirts of the village. It was one that I had drooled over after putting our flyer through the door.

We turned off the main street into a quiet side lane and, as we rounded a curve, there stood the cottage I remembered in all its crooked glory, looking even better than before. It was seventeenth century with three floors, its uppermost level sporting deep dormer windows with not one straight line anywhere in sight. Despite its three hundred-plus years of settling and warping, it had a great feeling of solidity, and glowed from the sun's reflection off its honey-coloured local stone. The roof line dipped slightly from the many years of supporting the original slate tiles. The untrimmed wisteria and roses rambling above its front door and windows gave it just the right blowsy look. Fittingly, it was called Wisteria Cottage.

As we stepped inside, I was suddenly aware of a 'this-is-the-one' feeling, the exact same emotion I'd had about the Kelmscott cottage we had tried to purchase previously. I gripped Randy's arm to steady my trembling. There was no hallway and the front door opened directly into a very small living room typical of cottages of this era. The original floor of uneven flagstones was uncovered except for a Persian rug in front of the inglenook fireplace, with logs piled in two alcoves on either side.

We were greeted warmly by the owners, James and Jane Rumore, who showed us over the cottage. They were tiny, elderly and frail. The ground floor didn't take long to view because it was so small. Next to the living room was a kitchen, also with a fireplace. Everything looked well ordered and a cleaning lady was busily polishing brass as we looked around.

I noticed that, although Randy needed to duck to get through the front door, the ceiling of the cottage was a comfortable couple of inches above his head. Because this property had three floors, it was a cut above the ordinary worker's cottages and, consequently, constructed with slightly higher ceilings.

Next, Jane, who seemed to be taking the lead in showing the property, took us upstairs. This meant climbing the charming circular stone staircase which seemed to have been hewn out of a wall next to the fireplace. Upstairs were two small bedrooms and a bathroom, all in good condition. Then, we climbed another circular staircase which led to the top floor.

'This is what we use for the master bedroom and we divided the space and put in a bathroom,' said Jane, who was followed by James, puffing and panting as he reached the top stair.

As we entered, both Randy and I stopped in our tracks.

'Ohhh, Randy!' I exclaimed.

'Ahhh,' said Randy at the exact same moment.

It was perfect. The exposed crooked attic beams, their colour pale grey and chalky-looking with age, framed the room, creating the cosiest possible atmosphere. The dormer windows looked out over a stunning view across the garden, tree tops, and fields, dotted with sheep, beyond. Far in the distance, a river meandered through the landscape, its surface glittering in the late afternoon sun. An old wrought-iron bedstead, positioned opposite this spectacular view, stood on wide-planked oak floorboards scattered with several Persian rugs.

Now I was trembling from head to foot and Randy looked pale. We stood there in a daze for several moments before I noticed a door, barely waist high, leading to another room.

'What's that?' I asked.

'The bathroom is through there,' said Jane.

'But it's like Alice in Wonderland,' I said, 'you'd have to bend double to get through it.'

'Yes,' said James, 'it's too low but that could be fixed. We've been meaning to get it done, but it's quite a to-do because a beam will have to be supported to put in a proper door frame. We're used to it now.'

James and Jane were short enough that they could just duck to get through this door frame and into the bathroom, but Randy and I had to bend down considerably. Once we entered, we were stunned by the beauty of the room. Again the exposed beams, gnarled with age, gave it masses of character. An ancient, claw-foot bath was mounted on a dais in the centre. This made it the perfect height for anyone who was bathing to catch the same spectacular view as in the bedroom. It would be wonderful to have a long soak in this tub with nothing to do but drink a cocktail and take in the vista.

As we went back downstairs to the small living room, a thought flashed through my mind. The living room really is too small. Is this the tragic flaw?

'Of course, this is far too small for a living room,' said Jane, as if reading my thoughts. 'We had intended to extend into the barn.'

She took us back out into the garden and showed us a stone barn that was at right angles to the cottage, and indicated the narrow space between the two.

'You could have a contractor join the two buildings together and make a good-sized living room here. It could be built of the old Cotswold stone and there would be space for a cloakroom and some storage too.'

'Would we be able to get a permit for that if we buy?' I asked.

'We've already obtained planning permission from the county council. Of course, we had to get plans done first, but we would throw them in for free. If we moved they would be no more use to us.'

Randy and I both realised at the same time that the tragic flaw had suddenly disappeared. Carrying out this work would make the cottage absolute perfection. It would have everything on our wish list.

'If you have the permission and the plans why didn't you build the living room?' asked Randy.

'We've been putting it off. It's such a disruption,' said James. 'You see I have asthma and...' Jane interrupted him.

'We were just starting to think about doing that when we realised the stairs are already getting too much for us, didn't we dear?' asked Jane, as she looked meaningfully at her husband.

'I see... so that's why you want to sell now?'

'Well... I actually don't want to sell,' said James.

Randy and I froze.

'What do you mean?' I asked.

'We've looked around a bit and we haven't liked anything we've seen,' replied James, 'let's face it, we're never going to find anything as nice as this. Look at that field view. The stairs are a bit much, but we'll be alright for a while.'

'But you invited us to come and view it,' I quietly wailed.

'That was my wife,' said James grumpily.

'Yes,' explained Jane, 'I saved your flyer and I invited you over because I think we need to get serious about selling.' The couple glared at each other for a second or two and icicles seemed to form in the air. It was suddenly obvious that we were in the middle of a marital tug-of-war.

'I'm confused. Are you selling or not?' I asked.

'Well, we will be when we find a place that James likes. I do apologise for asking you to view the cottage under these circumstances. I really should have told you the situation before I asked you to come. I picked out your flyer because you say on it that you don't have to sell a house first and if it worked out we wouldn't all be in a chain of other buyers and sellers.'

'Do you intend to put it with an estate agent on the open market?' Randy asked.

'No,' replied Jane, 'we could do that and I know we wouldn't have any trouble selling it, but we don't want a lot of people tramping through the house viewing it, so we prefer to sell it privately.'

She looked meaningfully at James again before she turned to us and continued.

'If you can wait, we could make an agreement to offer it to you before anybody else. That is if you are interested.'

Randy and I looked at each other and nodded and then turned to Jane.

'Yes,' we said together. But my heart sank and Randy looked crestfallen.

After that we were shown the garden which had a lily pond and was well stocked with mature plants. Because it backed onto a field it appeared to extend for miles. We sat outside on the York stone patio and had drinks while we discussed a purchase price. It was higher than we wanted to go, but since it wasn't actually on the market there was no point in negotiating.

As we talked we realised that the cottage had yet another thing in its favour. The garden was in the right position to catch the sunset, and on this particular evening there was a glorious one that spread across the sky, bathing the rolling hills beyond the garden in a shimmering pink glow.

The next day we fluctuated between thrilled excitement and utter despair. The stars had aligned; we had found our dream cottage but couldn't have it.

'We might wait forever before these sellers see another home that they like,' I said to Randy.

'I don't think we should wait,' he replied, 'let's find something bad about the whole thing so that we can cross this cottage off our list.'

We made a list of pros and cons, and the only negative thing on it was the construction that would have to be done to create a larger living room.

'Perhaps there's something wrong with the village that it's in,' I suggested. 'Maybe that's where we'll find the tragic flaw?'

We drove back to the village the next day but when we explored it we found it was, in fact, charming. It was a hot day and the sun made everything sparkle. There was a seventeenth century pub that served delicious food in the village. We made sure of that by having a lunch of scallops on a bed of *mista* with caramelised walnuts and Randy pronounced the local Hook Norton beer the best.

The village also had a shop, staffed by volunteer village residents, which sold all the basics. There was a Norman church with a cool and peaceful interior and a school. Best of all, the village was bypassed by heavy traffic. Also, there were very few modern buildings, as this was a conservation area and everything was well kept and neat.

On our way out of the village we drove slowly by Wisteria Cottage and I started to blub. I wanted that cottage so much I ached.

To cheer me up Randy took me to Mickleton in the very far north of Gloucestershire close to the border of Worcestershire and Warwickshire. This tiny village, three miles north of Chipping Campden, lies just beneath the Cotswold Edge and has an interesting church with a fourteenth century tower and spire and a very unusual seventeenth century double-decker porch. We took the rigorous circular walk that led up the hill to Kiftsgate Court Gardens. This fabulously romantic garden, which is open to the public, is a must-see for any visitor to the Cotswolds.

Kiftsgate was created by three generations of women gardeners. Heather Muir established the garden in the 1920s followed by Diany Binny from 1950 and finally by Anne Chambers with help from her husband. The terrace garden is so lush and imaginatively planted with gorgeous vistas across the matchless Cotswolds landscape that I found it very hard to leave.

The following morning, Randy reminded me of what our friend Sandra had advised.

'Even when you find a cottage you like, don't stop looking. You'll need backups as it's so easy for things to go wrong.'

A mill cottage near Lechlade

As if on cue, the phone rang and one of our estate agents gave us the particulars of a cottage for sale in Buscot near Lechlade. I made an appointment to see it the next day even though I was feeling quite hopeless. To cheer me up Randy arranged a day out built around the viewing appointment. He made it all a surprise – a sort of magical mystery tour and I wasn't to ask any questions – just enjoy the day as it unfolded.

First off we drove to Lechlade for breakfast. This small market town was once a busy stop on the Thames and Severn Canal but now its boats are used only for pleasure. Its two bridges cross the Thames and one is charmingly called Ha'penny Bridge with its tollhouse overlooking the boatyard at the southern end of town. There is a fine Perpendicular parish church and boats can be rented from the banks of the Thames by The Trout pub.

Randy's efforts to get me out of my funk continued as he handed me the morning paper to read as we set off on our drive over to Buscot. He had marked an item he thought might amuse me. It was a picture of Elton John who had arrived at a royal event in an outfit that was very similar to Queen Elizabeth's. I think English newspapers are the best.

As we arrived at the Buscot Estate and drove through the entrance of the 55-acre park that surrounds it, I found it easy to imagine what it would have been like to live in this beautiful place in earlier times. We drove slowly past a tree-bordered lake and an elaborate water garden to reach this grand Palladian-style Italianate house, built in the 1770s by Edward Loveden Townsend.

As we toured Buscot House we found that a subsequent owner, the first Lord Faringdon, had filled it with fine furniture and paintings by Rembrandt, Murillo and Reynolds. The pre-Raphaelite artist Edward Burne-Jones's paintings had been added to the collection at a later date. In 1956, the Buscot Park estate was bequeathed to the National Trust. The current Lord Faringdon lives at the park and administers the estate on behalf of the Trust.

It was a lovely surprise for me to be taken on this tour by Randy as I knew little about this stately home and had to admit that, much as I enjoyed seeing the house, the gardens proved to be an even bigger treat. Sir Harold Peto, the leading light in Italian-revival garden design, had been commissioned to create the water garden to link the house and the lake. We stood outside and saw how the water garden led our gaze to a perfect vista, starting with a sculptural fountain and on through to a distant lake reflecting the trees surrounding it.

The Peto gardens are world famous, and Randy and I had already enjoyed visiting another by this same designer – Ilford Gardens near Bath. This one at Buscot, however, was on an even grander scale. We spent a long time strolling around the various sunlit garden rooms including the 'citrus bowl', the magnificent 'four seasons walled garden', the 'swinging garden' which featured wooden swings suspended from their frames, and the circular 'tumulus garden'.

We took a turn around the lake, walked the length of the water garden and lingered on the humpback bridge until Randy led me to another section of the grounds. To my joy this was an area of the grounds devoted to the growing of soft fruit, flowers and vegetables that the visitors could pick themselves and pay for by the pound. We had a great time, in the hot sunshine, picking pounds of ripe strawberries, blackberries and raspberries from the rows of ripened fruit. These would make many jars of jam.

'This is making me hungry. What should we do about lunch?' I asked Randy after a while.

'I have an idea about that. I'll take the fruit to the car – I brought a cooler for it – and be back in a minute.'

He returned shortly with another surprise. He had secretly packed a delicious lunch which he spread out in the picnic area that overlooked the fruit and vegetable farm. We feasted on a left-over lamb *roulard* with olives and figs that Randy had cooked the night before and was now even better cold. This was accompanied by a cucumber and mint Greek *tzatziki* which was packed in ice and perfect for a hot day. We tore off some chunks of *ciabatta* to go with everything, and sipped a crisp, cold *Pinot Grigio*. Naturally, we had a heap of freshly picked fruit for dessert.

There were few other visitors there and it was quiet enough to hear the bees buzzing in the garden as we relaxed on the grass.

'What a great magical mystery tour. This has been the best,' I said to Randy.

'What makes you think it's over?' he replied.

'There's more?'

'Yes, but first we should see the cottage for sale.'

We went off to our appointment with me hoping that lightning would strike twice. Perhaps there was another cottage out there that would fit the bill. But it was not to be. This property for sale, on the outskirts of Buscot village was separated from a busy lane by only a few yards and, instead of the usual Cotswold stone; it was made of an ugly flint. In addition, the ceilings were so low that Randy had to crouch in every room. There was absolutely no comparison with the wonderful Wisteria Cottage, but before I could get glum about it Randy took me off on a walk to nearby Buscot Weir which is next to a lock on the Thames.

We crossed the river by one of the two footbridges and meandered along the Thames Path enjoying the sight of the boats drifting towards Lechlade. Next, we found the Church of St Mary's in the village and explored it. The *Domesday Book* lists Buscot as one of the most valuable fisheries on the Thames. This reminded me that I had seen the phrase 'mentioned in the *Domesday Book*' in the description of many properties including cottages, old mills, churches and other public buildings, but I didn't really know exactly what it was. I had read up on it and found that the *Domesday Book* had been commissioned by William the Conqueror in December 1085 and contains records of almost 14,000 settlements in English counties. The *Domesday Book* (actually two books) is kept in a chest in London's Public Record Office in Kew, London. It includes a survey of the lands in each of the counties: the possessions of the magnates, their lands, their homes, their men, both bonded and free, those living in huts and those owning their own houses or land.

It is thought that the primary purpose of the book was to facilitate the collection of taxes. It also states how many ploughs, horses and other animals there were, and also the payments due from each and every estate. The fund of money collected was called *Danegeld* and was used to buy off the marauding Danish armies.

No mention is made of St Mary's Church in the *Domesday Book*, although it is thought that the church probably existed at the time the book was compiled. St Mary's was later enlarged during the fifteenth century. A rare medieval bell frame is still in the tower of the church as is a fourteenth century bell. I picked up a booklet in the church and read out a passage to Randy. It was about the previous owners of the Buscot Estate, but somehow it read like a Monty Python sketch.

'Edward Loveden Townsend, a descendent of Edward Loveden and Margaret Pryse, inherited the Buscot Estate from his great uncle on condition that he drop the name Townsend. Confusingly he became Edward Loveden Loveden. Meanwhile his son Pryse Loveden took his mother's family name in 1798 and so became Pryse Pryse. His son, also Pryse, resumed the name Loveden.

After we had chuckled about this we admired the Good Shepherd stained-glass window which was designed in 1892 by the same Edward Burne-Jones whose paintings hang in Buscot House.

We ambled back and, as it was now early evening, I thought we were making for the car, but instead Randy took me back into the grounds of Buscot for yet another surprise. A group of people were gathering on the front terrace of the house and sherry and *hors d'oeuvre* were being handed around. I happily joined in, wondering what was going to happen next. Randy wasn't telling and, after chatting to a few interesting people, we were all led inside Buscot House to what turned out to be an exquisite sixty-seat, jewel box of a theatre. I had no idea that there was one there.

The theatre quickly filled and everybody was buzzing with chatter but quieted down when the curtain rose.

'Mud, mud, glorious mud, nothing quite like it for cooling the blood.'

Beginning with the *Hippopotamus Song*, two extremely talented actors gave us an evening of the music and songs of Flanders and Swann. I was thrilled as I adore their tunes, among them *Madeira M'dear*, and *The Gnu*. This show was perfectly suited to the intimate theatre.

There was no end to Randy's surprises as, during the intermission, the entire audience returned to the terrace where a picnic dinner of poached salmon and Caesar salad accompanied by some delicious wine was served to everybody in the audience. We were joined by the two performers of the show and over dinner chatted to them about the relative merits of acting in England, as opposed to 'treading the boards' on our side of the Atlantic. It all seemed very civilised to have dinner in the interval; I think every show should do it. By now darkness was closing in, and from the terrace Buscot House looked wonderful in the floodlights that illuminated its classical outlines.

A thatched cottage near Burford

After dinner, the audience and the performers, wine glasses still in hand, returned for the second half of the show which turned out to be even livelier than the first. My clever husband had known about this performance for a while and had planned it as a surprise treat. When he realised that the cottage viewing was to be in the same area he seized the opportunity of putting it all together, with the tour of the house and a picnic, to make the perfect outing. It had done the trick – I was happy again.

Over the next few days there were no new cottage viewings and my thoughts returned repeatedly to Wisteria Cottage. It just felt so right.

'Randy, I can't stand it. I can't get Wisteria Cottage out of my mind.'

'No. Neither can I.'

'But how long can we wait?'

Randy crunched some numbers and worked out that we had six weeks' money left before we had to start dipping into the cottage fund for living expenses.

'It's going to all slip away,' I said, 'if we run out of money before the Wisteria Cottage owners find another home. The last time I talked to them they hadn't viewed anything new at all.'

'There must be something we can do to hurry things along,' said Randy

'I've got it!' I yelled with a burst of inspiration.

'Is it catching?' asked Randy.

'We find them a new home, then we can buy Wisteria Cottage.'

'Really? In that case why don't we just find ourselves another cottage?'

'No, we'll find them a barn. That's much easier.'

'I don't get it.'

'Lots of the farmers are converting their barns into homes.'

'Yes, but I wouldn't like to live in one.'

'Exactly, neither would I. We'll find one for James and Jane and then move into their cottage.'

'How do we know if they'll want to live in one?'

'Remember, James can't manage the stairs anymore and a barn, if it's a small one, is really the only kind of building in the countryside that is often just one storey.'

'Wow, you're right! This might work.'

'It's got to have a field view, though. He mentioned that.'

'Trust you to find a way.'

'We'll see; we're not there yet.'

That afternoon I telephoned Jane at Wisteria Cottage. Luckily she could talk freely as James was outside in the garden. She thought my plan was terrific but warned me that it would be best to keep it between ourselves. She had no objection to buying a converted barn and sounded immensely relieved that I was going to help them find one with no stairs.

'He's so stubborn. His asthma is bad and his balance is going as well,' she said, referring to her husband.

'We have to do something about all this soon. We just don't have the energy to do much looking ourselves and our children are busy with their families.'

I spent a long time calling all my estate agents and contacts with my new requirements: a small, converted barn or outbuilding of one storey, with two or three bedrooms and a field view.

Strangely enough the view was the problem. I always think of a barn being in a field so it must have a view. This is not always the case, however, as many of the converted barns have their views restricted by other outbuildings on a farm. We looked at a few conversions, but there were all kinds of problems and I knew these would not be acceptable.

'The actors and writers' strike looks like it is ending. That's the rumour anyway.'

Our friends had called from Los Angeles with this news the following day. If it did end we would be in a real quandary. It would be tempting to go back to earn more money, especially if Wisteria Cottage turned out to be more than we could manage at present, but then we wouldn't be around to look for a barn.

It seemed that we would be between a rock and a hard place, and I felt like tearing my hair out. But Randy, calm as ever, took me off to dinner at the charming little pub that was in the same village as Wisteria Cottage.

'Let's act as if we own the cottage already,' he said, remembering my shrink Sara's instructions.

In the pub we mingled with some farmers and field workers at the bar as we got our drinks. One farmer type was looking at us thoughtfully as he listened to Randy ordering our beer.

'Were you them that was looking at Wisteria Cottage?' he asked.

'Yes,' said Randy, 'how did you know?'

'Accent you got. Stands out a bit,' replied the farmer.

'News sure travels fast in a small village,' said Randy.

'That's it; secrets don't last long 'round 'ere.'

Randy and I laughed.

'I's Dan,' he said extending his hand. We introduced ourselves.

'My sister is thems cleaner lady see,' he continued, 'I bet yous still lookin' as she don't see 'em as movin' soon.'

'Yes, we are,' I replied.

'Well, I ain't got a cottage to sell you but on me farm I do 'ave a barn.'

Randy and I almost dropped our drinks. We looked at the barn the same day. It was in the next village and wasn't on the market yet. It was Cotswold stone, only one storey, with one large bedroom and one smaller one and, glory be, it had a field view. The farm was well kept and just on the outskirts of the village. The remodelling that was being done on the barn was its only drawback, as this was not yet finished.

'How long before it's done?' asked Randy.

'Three months or could be four. Depends on the weather,' Dan replied.

I called Jane and asked her to come over immediately and while we waited we explained our situation to Dan.

Jane really liked the barn. Dan said she could customise some of the fittings which made her very happy. It was in the right price range but, of course, now she would have to persuade her husband to move.

'It ticks all the boxes,' she said as she left.

On the drive back, Randy pointed out that if we bought Wisteria Cottage now the completion period would be up just as the barn's remodelling was finished. It would all fit together perfectly.

'That would be great but how can we do that? I don't think we have enough money in the cottage fund,' I wailed.

'We don't need all the money at the beginning. Just the deposit. We don't have to produce the big down-payment until the final stages of buying the cottage. If we can bring the purchase price down a bit and hop back to

Los Angeles and work to get some more dough, we've got a chance. Remember the lease our tenants have in Los Angeles is up soon.'

I thought it was too risky. We could lose our deposit doing this.

'Hooray, the strike is over! Come back to Los Angeles you two. We miss you.'

We found this message from our friends on our answering machine when we returned to our digs and, in addition, a letter with a cheque in it from a travel magazine. My article must have finally reached the top of the slush pile in the editor's office, as it had been published. There was also a note asking me to submit more articles.

Randy and I took these two pieces of good news as a sign. We would go ahead with the plan that he had suggested. But of course everything hinged on James wanting the barn. Would he like it or not? This was a real cliff-hanger.

Carving from Chavenage House, Tetbury

Ten

IT DOESN'T GET MUCH BETTER THAN THIS
Tetbury, Cheltenham, Thrupp

'Ice in your drink?'

The flight attendant pushed her drinks cart further down the aisle of the plane obscuring my last view of England as Randy and I flew back to Los Angeles. We toasted each other.

'To Wisteria Cottage,' we said together.

After a big struggle, Jane had managed to get James to view the barn and he had grudgingly conceded that it had a fine field view, and ticked a lot of boxes for him too. Jane worked on him to sell up and buy the barn. We had decided to return to Los Angeles and a few days before our departure we heard from Jane.

'Last night James's breathing was so bad he couldn't make it up the stairs to the bedroom. Finally this made him see the light.'

On our very last day in England, we had negotiated for Wisteria Cottage. The final figure was reduced a bit and a sale price was agreed upon. The deal was contingent on the purchase of the barn going through and on us getting a mortgage.

When we returned to Los Angeles we took out a second mortgage on our house, a large chunk of which was going to be used for our down-payment, if we got Wisteria Cottage. We still didn't have all we needed but, luckily, Randy was offered a slew of work and I busily put together several articles for the travel magazine that had bought my earlier one.

To help avoid a repeat of our gazumping experience earlier in the year, we stayed in close touch with both our solicitor and our mortgage broker in England and hurried them along as much as possible. If everything went forward as planned, it was still going to be touch and go. Would we have enough money for the down-payment on Wisteria Cottage by the time it was needed?

While I was waiting to hear if my articles had sold, other work was coming in very slowly, so I called up my theatrical agent and told him to lower the bar right down to the ground – I would take any job that paid money.

'Did you like my song and dance, children? I'm the Birthday Bear.'

'I don't believe you.'

'Why is that, birthday girl?'

'My name's Samantha, you're not a bear, you're a person. You've missed some make-up under your chin.'

My agent had taken me at my word and now I was performing on one of the bottom rungs of the showbiz ladder – as the entertainer at a rich kid's birthday party. The money offered was surprisingly good, however, so I couldn't turn it down.

The party was being held in a function room in a swanky Beverly Hills hotel, and the moment I entered I encountered about three dozen children who immediately crowded around me, pushing and shoving, in their overdressed finery.

Their heavily bejewelled mothers, equally overdressed in insanely expensive designer outfits, were sitting at the back of the room, yakking away ninety to the dozen and drinking cocktails as they paid absolutely no attention to their children or me.

I was wearing an ill-fitting bear suit that was way too hot. Especially, since I had just opened my act with a rousing song and dance to the tune of *The Teddy Bears' Picnic*. My bear costume barely fit around my head and I had apparently missed a patch of the brown make-up applied all over my uncovered face and neck. Now the observant, over-privileged, eight-year-old birthday princess seated in front of me was making sure I knew this.

'Samantha, thank you for pointing out that I've missed some make-up. Now tell this bear what you are getting for your birthday.'

'A Vera Wang dress and Manolo Blahnik shoes.'

'Goodness, I didn't know that those designers made outfits for little girls.'

'They don't really, but mine are being specially made for me. And I'm getting a laptop and a real diamond bracelet. Do you have a diamond bracelet?'

'No, I don't. What would a bear want with a diamond bracelet? Ouch!'

I was suddenly aware of a sharp pain. I looked down to see a little boy hammering my foot with a heavy ray gun.

'Hey, stop that!'

'My name's Tristram. My uncle owns this hotel and I can do anything I want,' said the little boy as he hammered even harder.

'You're hurting my toes.'

'If you were a real bear you would have claws, not toes,' said Samantha.

'OK, you win, I'm not a real bear.'

Another, more innocent, child started to cry. I made an attempt to cheer her up by telling a few kiddie jokes and next I sang and danced another tune, limping a little from my injured foot. I tried to get the kids to join in.

'You, little girl, the one with the mink fur trim on your dress, would you like to sing with me?'

'No!'

One by one they all refused. So I sang by myself. When I had finished Tristram piped up again.

'When are you going to make us laugh?'

'Never, at this rate. You're the toughest audience I've played since the St Jude's Home for Retired Manic Depressives.'

'Then I'm going to tell my Mommy not to pay you,' said Samantha.

'Now children, you wouldn't want a big bear to lose its temper would you? And roll on you and give you such a big bear hug that you almost couldn't breathe?'

'No,' said the kids, slightly intimidated.

'Good, then I'll pretend that I'm a bear and you pretend you're all normal children and you like me and we'll get along just fine.'

In the distance I saw the event coordinator who had hired me approaching with my cheque in her hand. To make it look as if I had earned my money I flung myself into an incredibly energetic song and dance in a final attempt to engage the kids. But going this much over the top in my bear suit was a mistake. My temperature soared to about a thousand degrees and I suddenly felt faint. I just managed to tear off the furry bear's head before collapsing on the floor, semi-conscious. The kids must have thought the bear had torn its own head off because they screamed hysterically. The event coordinator, very nervous that the mothers would be upset, shouted at the kids to follow her so that she could quiet them down in another room. Follow her they did, and I remained on the floor while thirty-six screaming children stomped on my prone body as they scrambled after her.

While my bruises were still fading, we heard from Jane that, after several complications, a deal had been worked out for the barn. A few days later we were told that the inspection on Wisteria Cottage had been satisfactory. These major hurdles had been overcome, with only one more to go. Our mortgage.

We ran into a lot of difficulties with the fact that we were applying for a mortgage from overseas. Poor Randy was working night and day. By day on television shows, and at night he would plough through more mortgage documents than it is possible to imagine. All these would be emailed to our English mortgage broker who was terrific. After a couple of months of great struggle, he announced that we had a loan. In theory, that is, as we had to come up with our down-payment money before it got funded. It was going to be a close run thing.

I worked everything that was offered to me and then I started to sell my bits of jewellery. We still didn't have quite enough, but two days before the deadline, I sold another article and Randy got a big re-run cheque on a network show.

Whew! We just made it under the wire. Some more paperwork got wrangled, and then our broker called.

'You have a mortgage for Wisteria Cottage,' he announced victoriously.

'Wow, wahooo! Yes!'

'We did it!'

'Is it really true?'

'Yes,' said our broker, 'now all you have to do is complete.'

'What?' said Randy.

'Close escrow,' I interpreted.

After all this, it had finally happened. We were stunned. We opened some champagne and toasted each other as we looked at photos of Wisteria Cottage. I actually had a little blub of relief, and Randy went to bed at 9 o'clock to catch up on his sleep.

That following week we threw a party to celebrate finally reaching our goal. When our friends saw the shots of Wisteria Cottage they all wanted to come and stay. We had another six weeks or so before Wisteria Cottage formally became ours. This date was to be set as soon as the barn was finished and would bring us around to late spring when the television studios more or less shut down for a hiatus. As soon as production closed down, we planned to go to England and take possession of our cottage.

But there was still one more wrinkle. It was raining in England. The longer it rained the slower the progress on the barn. We looked at long-range weather forecasts on the Internet. We prayed to the rain gods. We even called the farmer's contractor in England. He promised to hurry things up as much as possible.

Meanwhile, we were still working all the hours we could for money. This time it would go towards furniture. I had a few pieces that relatives and friends were storing for me from when I had lived in England years before, but we would need much more.

After a couple of weeks, the skies cleared in England and work on the exterior of the barn resumed. We breathed a sigh of relief.

The next five weeks flew by. With one more week to go before we travelled, we got word that Jane and James had signed the completion forms at their solicitor's office and had moved into their barn. Wisteria Cottage was ours!

We were too busy packing to do any more celebrating and pretty soon we were on the plane. In England we drove straight to the solicitor's office to pick up the keys to our new home. Next, we drove directly to it. As we rounded the curve of the quiet side lane in which it stood, Wisteria Cottage looked even lovelier than I remembered, solidly sitting there in the warm sun. The roses over the door were in early bloom and looked even blowsier than before, with a scattering of petals piled on the grass below.

We walked inside and wandered around the empty rooms in awe. It was ours. The cottage looked much bigger without furniture. We climbed the circular stone staircases to the top floor and drank in the wonderful view. We went to the barn and danced around. We ran around in the garden and talked to the cows in the field beyond.

A bed-and-breakfast room at the local pub became our home for the first couple of weeks and we had lots of fun buying second-hand furniture and decorating. My sister had been storing my cottage hope chest that I had gathered over the last few years and we picked this up. It consisted of some pieces of furniture, including a Thonet bentwood rocking chair, one of the first antiques I had ever bought, a brass oil lamp and various other items including old china, lace tablecloths and linens.

We purchased dozens of bargains for our cottage at various antique shops and car boot sales in the Cotswolds and used this opportunity to explore parts of this region that were new to us. We made a day out of it, finding an area that was known for antiques or car boot sales and after that selecting a hike nearby in one of our pub walk books. We would hike in the morning, have a pub lunch, and shop in the afternoon. In this way we had a wonderful trip to the ancient town of Tetbury which has twenty or thirty great antique shops. These shops are grouped around a seventeenth century Town Hall which is supported by three rows of Tuscan pillars. Nearby, is Gumstool Hill where Tetbury's famous Woolsack Races are held. Teams race down to the cattle market and back up the hill from the Crown Inn to the Royal Oak each carrying a 65lb sack of wool. This is part of the Tetbury Festival – also known as Woolsack Day.

Tetbury's Church of St Mary is well worth a visit with its beautifully proportioned interior featuring panelled galleries, Perpendicular windows and box pews. Tetbury has the added bonus of being close to Princes Charles' country home Highgrove. In the summer months Prince Charles' garden is open to the public. We came back on a second occasion to tour the Highgrove garden which is extraordinarily beautiful. Highlights for me included a pergola with an apple walk, masses of different garden rooms of distinctive character and a walled garden sporting delicious looking climbing pear trees.

We discovered Cheltenham on our antique buying trips too. This town has an extensive car boot sale every Sunday and we would shop all morning followed by lunch in the Kings Arms pub in the quaint village of Prestbury on the outskirts of Cheltenham. After lunch we would explore, strolling around and taking in the Pittville Pump Room which houses Cheltenham's spa and the Regency architecture, much of which is grouped around the perfectly proportioned Promenade with its top-of-the-line shops and spacious walkways. There is a lot to see including the Neptune Fountain, the Montpellier Assembly Rooms the Imperial Gardens and St Mary's Church. A little further away is the Cheltenham Racecourse – where the Royal family is often seen watching the races, the John Dower building and the Gustav Holst Museum.

We also found a wonderful antique and second-hand furniture store in Thrupp near Stroud in Gloucestershire. This is not necessarily the prettiest town in the Cotswolds but it is a lovely drive through the surrounding countryside. Early records indicate that there was a cloth mill in Thrupp, dating from 1381, and it is also the site of the invention of the first lawn mower.

Randy concentrated on getting the kitchen set up. That was top priority. He took lessons from our friends Sandra and Jim on how to use an AGA. Friends and my family helped and within two weeks we had enough of the basics in place to move in.

Newborn calf in meadow near Burford

We packed our bags, paid our bill at the pub, and drove over to our new home. The sign that said Wisteria Cottage seemed particularly welcoming as we carried our bags over the threshold of the front door.

Over the next few weeks everything else we needed seemed to come together really easily. In between finding furniture and fixing things, we would take a rest in an old wooden seat in the garden. It caught the sun in the mornings and we would have breakfast out there and get to know the cows when they put their heads over the low fence. On other occasions we delighted in being able to climb over this fence into the field beyond and hike to the next village. It was wonderful to just walk directly from our garden and on and on through fields of shoulder-high crops or grazing sheep. On one of our hikes we followed a river and couldn't believe our luck when we discovered that it widened out to a swimming hole. It was surrounded by trees and deserted except for occasional visits from the village kids. We took picnics there on hot days and it was great to have a place to swim. The more we explored the fields and villages surrounding us, the more we appreciated how fortunate our choice had been.

Finally it was time to plan the thing I had been longing to do since the beginning of our cottage odyssey – have a house-warming party. I had a fantasy about how it would be; just like the ones I had read about in travel books. After the remodelling of the Tuscan villa or the French farmhouse, there would be the obligatory final chapter that would describe the perfect party. The great groaning tables of food, the merry villagers gathering to wish the new owners well, as friends and family turn up from all over with armfuls of house-warming gifts. Everything goes according to plan; everybody bonds and has a rousing good time as the camaraderie oozes like syrup. We were going to do the same: serve up wonderful food and drink and invite friends, family and half the village, so what could possibly go wrong?

By now we had met some of our neighbours and they helpfully told us that for a small donation we could borrow all the things from the village hall that we needed for a party. We were given the key and collected chairs, tables, plates, glasses and cutlery.

Randy started planning the food and I got on the phone to invite guests. We needed good weather for the party as our tiny living room couldn't possibly accommodate the number of people invited. It would be a while before we could afford to convert our barn into a larger living room that would be ideal for a big crowd.

We shopped and cooked and cooked and shopped. But it was a labour of love because it was all happening in our cottage.

It rained all week leading up to the party. We prayed again to the rain gods for it to stop just for the Saturday. And Friday night at midnight the rain stopped right on cue. The sun shone the next day and everything dried out.

Randy had outdone himself on the menu. It was to be a buffet, so it all had to be fork food. He had made the lightest possible salmon mousse with *crème fraîche*. He had used a fish mould, and the finished dish looked magnificent. For another dish he had taken boneless organic chicken thighs and marinated them in a honey mustard mixture that Tony the butcher had made up for him. He par-cooked them in the oven and finished them off on a *mesquite*-chip barbecue. This made them incredibly tasty and succulent, so different from the usual dried-out, wooden barbecue chicken. These he cooked in the afternoon, to be warmed up later for the party.

Another dish consisted of small roasted sweet potatoes still in their skins, cooked and then broken open and drizzled with brandy butter and herbs. My favourite taste treat of the party was a lamb *roulade* stuffed with chestnut and *tapenade*. For this dish, Randy boned a leg of lamb and cut it very thin and then flattened it with a mallet. He rolled it around the dressing and tied it with string. When it was cooked he let it cool and cut it into thin slices. It held together in circles and the lamb was so tender it could be cut with the edge of a fork.

A second lamb dish was cooked with lavender and tiny white onions. We cut the lamb into small chunks for forking and reheated it for the party. Instead of potatoes, Randy served parsnips mashed and whipped with butter, salt and pepper. This was sprinkled with cheese and heated under the grill until a crisp top formed. He cooked chicken breasts in a *béchamel* sauce, and another tasty dish, braised leeks in butter and lemon. There was local asparagus and Randy's Caesar salad, one of his best, with shaved fresh parmesan and anchovies.

I made my signature salad dish which I had enjoyed in the south of France. Starting with fresh organic tomatoes sliced very thin, I add garlic, chopped red onion and fresh basil. This is marinated in olive oil and aged balsamic vinegar. I arrange it on an oval serving dish and put layers and layers of tomatoes on top of a border of basil leaves. I add more basil to the onions and garlic and sprinkle this on top of the tomatoes.

We served everything with fresh baguettes, Randy's home-made red onion marmalade, a freshly grated horseradish and mayonnaise mixture with a hot red-wine reduction sauce to go with the lamb. For drinks there was champagne, wine and club soda, and I made my favourite drink which is lavender lemonade.

A dear friend made us her trifle cake, a cross between an English trifle and a gateau, loaded with masses of red cherries and liberal amounts of Rémy Martin brandy. It was so delicious and the brandy fumes so strong that I was glad no naked flames were anywhere nearby. I was resentful that I would have to share any of it with the other party guests.

We prepared as much of the food ahead of time as possible before the party, but even so it was more than a little hectic on the day. Randy worked at warp speed in the last hour and we had everything under control with only moments to spare.

The weather, which had become steadily warmer throughout the day, looked good enough to set out our borrowed village-hall tables and chairs in the garden on the York stone patio – all with that fabulous field view.

Guests starting arriving at six o'clock, bringing some dishes they had contributed to the party. The trifle cake was carried in, wobbling mouth-wateringly in a covered dish, and was placed on the buffet table on the patio. My family, several sets of neighbours, and a bunch of villagers crowded in together, followed by the Brigadier and his wife and Sandra and Jim. Pat and William arrived with Bosun their dog. They had brought the dog with the promise that he would stay put in our garage for the duration of the party. Next, my friend Rita, who had been the contact for our mortgage broker, arrived. She had driven from London with him and his girlfriend. After this came Michael our actor friend, and following him some other friends from another village piled in, with Jane and James arriving last.

All the guests mingled on the patio with drinks and, after a tour of the cottage, dug into the salmon mousse. Everybody seemed to like what they ate and saw, and ooh'd and ahh'd in particular over the view. We served up more dishes and were happy to see that the guests were going gaga over the food. Also everybody seemed to be having a good time and great shouts of laughter were coming from the table where all the actors had congregated.

The guests were astonished as we heated up dishes and added more and more to the spread on the buffet table. They got quite lyrical about the local lamb which had turned out exceptionally well. When the red onion marmalade was added, it was perfection.

Everybody was so satiated by the starter and entrée courses that we decided to hold off serving the trifle cake until after the sunset. As the sun dipped, it created spreading fingers of scarlet splendour above our field and the chatter faded out as the guests turned to enjoy it.

For the next half an hour they all sat, full and happy, while Randy sang and played lovely old songs from the 1930s and '40s on his ukulele. As the sun disappeared behind the distant trees, I sighed with contentment. Our little party had turned out just like the ones in the travel books. I was relishing the fact that we were home and dry with only the dessert to be served, when suddenly the mood was shattered by a loud explosion. Fireworks bloomed into a brilliant array of colours above us and we saw that they were coming from a house bordering an adjacent field. Bosun could be heard barking in the garage.

'Oh no, not again!' exclaimed Joe, one of our neighbours.

'What do you mean?' asked Randy.

'They must be having dinner guests at Barking Mad Manor over there. Every time they do, they have a firework display. At least it's a bit earlier tonight. Try sleeping through that lot.'

'Yes,' said another neighbour, 'he's known as Banger Beaumont around these parts. Can't keep his hands off the explosives. His son is worse. He digs up his potatoes by putting explosive charges in the ground.'

Another huge boom rent the air as a further spray of fireworks went up, but this time one of the rockets fell short and headed our way. We all ducked and dodged as it whizzed around the garden and finally extinguished itself with a fizzle in the lily pond. Insane barking could be heard from the garage together with the sound of splintering wood as Bosun, maddened by the fireworks, burst out of the side door of the garage and tore through the party dragging the leg of a work bench, to which he had been secured, behind him. Randy and I both realised at the same moment that he was heading straight for the buffet table holding the trifle cake.

We moved as one. Randy scooped up the cake and I held its glass lid on as Bosun pelted by us. But the leg of the work bench he was dragging after him hooked itself around the bottom of a serving table holding dishes and cutlery. This then banged into Randy and me. I had to let go of the lid of the trifle cake to keep my balance and Randy tripped and staggered juggling the cake which was slurping around inside its dish. The cover fell off and smashed to the ground, and Randy appeared to be going down too. I reached out to steady him and helped him regain his balance at the last possible second. Bosun, still determined to do battle with the pyrotechnics, had continued, pulling the serving table loaded with dishes after him. His mad dash towards the field caused it to tip over and the dishes and dessert bowls on top of it were dumped with a terrific crash on the York stone patio. Every dish was broken, but the trifle cake, held aloft by Randy, stayed intact. A great cheer went up from the guests at this spectacular save.

I hunted around and found a supply of paper dessert bowls and Randy victoriously served the trifle cake. It was so good that many of the guests had second helpings and it disappeared in record time with many justly deserved compliments.

As I handed around the coffee I realised that reality hadn't matched up to my fantasy. Instead of the perfectly organised celebrations that I had read about, the latter part of our party had turned into a chaotic slapstick farce, and in fact had proved just as completely unpredictable as the hunt for the cottage itself. But somehow everybody seemed quite happy.

Later, the last guest gone, Randy and I sat outside in the still, warm night.

'We've finally got the cottage and now it's been christened with the party. What a roller coaster ride it's been. In a way, I'm sorry it's over,' said Randy.

'Yes,' I replied, 'the laughs, the hard work, the crazy jobs making money for the cottage fund, the eccentric characters we've met – it's been pretty wild.'

'And the disappointments,' said Randy, 'remember how low we were when we lost the Kelmscott cottage?'

'Do I? It was heart wrenching.'

'Well, it's over now,' said Randy, 'we've finally won through and I'd like to make a toast to your mother for all her inspiration.'

'Yes. To dear Mum,' I replied.

We clinked our glasses then watched the moon rise, bathing Wisteria Cottage in its silvery glow.

'It's all been worth it hasn't it?' asked Randy.

'Oh, yes,' I replied, 'every twist and turn. Now all we have to do is finish converting that little barn in the garden into our living room and put in another bathroom.'

'Uh oh, could this be Toad's Wild Ride all over again?' asked Randy.

'Who knows?' I smiled.

'It doesn't matter' he said 'It doesn't get much better than this.'

Cotswolds Memoir

Visitor Guide

Here is an eclectic guide, by no means comprehensive, which represents my choices of the crème de la crème of inns, attractions and activities culled from ten years of research. A number of these entries describe little known gems from the off-the-beaten track Cotswolds that are well worth a visit and will take the adventurous explorer far from the madding crowd. This author has not received any endorsements for any of these entries.

BONUS

This guide includes the postcode for instant input in GPS or Sat Navs (often hard to find even on official websites) for all entries, plus a web address for more in-depth inquiries.

PLEASE NOTE

Visitors would be wise to check opening times and days of all activities before setting forth.

Official tourist websites and conservation information are at the end of this guide.

BARNS

GREAT COXWELL TITHE BARN,
Faringdon, Oxfordshire, SN7 7LZ

www.nationaltrust.org.uk

Impressive example of the expertise of Gothic carpenters. Only surviving part of 13th century grange that provided income for Beaulieu Abbey.

ASHLEWORTH TITHE BARN,
Ashleworth, Gloucestershire, GL19 4JA

www.nationaltrust.org.uk

Now National Trust. Built in 1481-1515. Ten bays. Outstanding example of medieval timber framing. Picturesque setting on banks of the River Severn.

BOATING

COTSWOLD BOAT HIRE,
Next to St John's Lock at the Trout Public House, Lechlade, Gloucestershire, GL7 3HA

www.cotswoldboat.co.uk

Day cruisers and small boats for the River Thames.

COTSWOLD COUNTRY PARK AND BEACH,
Cirencester, Gloucestershire, GL7 6DF

www.cotswoldcountrypark.co.uk

Pedal boats and row boats on a lake. Family fun.

CASTLES

SUDELEY CASTLE,
Winchcombe, Gloucestershire, GL54 5JD

www.sudeleycastle.co.uk

Once home of Henry VIII's wife Katherine Parr and Queen Elizabeth I. Restored and now the home of the Dent-Brocklehursts and Lady Ashcombe.

BERKELEY CASTLE,

Berkeley, Gloucestershire, GL13 9PJ

www.berkeley-castle.com

12th century Norman fortress with curtain wall. Built by Robert Fitzharding and is the most outstanding example of medieval domestic architecture in the country.

WARWICK CASTLE,

Warwick, Warwickshire, CV34 4QU

www.warwick-castle.com

1,000 years of history. Well constructed tableaux. Great Hall. State Rooms. Jousting. Trebuchet. Great day out with the kids. Peacock Garden. Gives Disney a run for its money.

CHURCHES

ADDERBURY,

St Mary the Virgin, Adderbury, Oxfordshire, OX17 3LP

www.adderbury-stmarys.com

A must-see. The biggest and most architecturally important church in the whole of Oxfordshire. Features an amazing frieze containing gargoyles playing medieval musical instruments. 12th century.

ST. GEORGE'S CHURCH,

Kelmscott, Oxfordshire, GL7 3HG

www.oxfordshirecotswolds.org

Almost completely unaltered since it was built. The artist, William Morris, saved this church from Victorian remodelling. Little known and well worth a visit are the red ochre wall paintings, scenes from the Old and New Testaments, painted in 1280, that adorn the North Chapel. Details in framed display alongside.

FARMING

COTSWOLDS FARM PARK,
Nr. Guiting Power, Cheltenham, Gloucestershire,
GL54 5UG
www.cotswoldfarmpark.co.uk
   Touch barn. Rare breeds. Camping. Family fun.

THE BUTTS FARM,
South Cerney, Cirencester, Gloucestershire, GL7 5QE
www.thebuttsfarmshop.com
   Visit the farm. Great for kids. Check for times. Terrific
shop too.

FOOD SHOPPING

DAYLESFORD FARMSHOP & CAFÉ,
Near Kingham, Gloucestershire, GL56 0YG
www.daylesfordorganic.com
   Award-winning shop, food comes fresh from their
farm. Vegetables, herbs, meat all organic. Deep pockets
needed but so worth it. Farm tours and walks.

MABYS DELICATESSAN,
Stow-in-the-Wold, Oxfordshire, GL54 1BN
www.localstore.co.uk
   All manner of exotic and hard-to-get-items. Ready-
made *haute cuisine* dishes.

THE BUTTS FARM SHOP,
South Cerney, Cirencester, Gloucestershire, GL7 5QE
www.thebuttsfarmshop.com
   Terrific shop. Meat bought by 10,000 people a year.

GARDENS AND ARBORETA

NATIONAL GARDEN SCHEME,

www.ngs.org.uk

A terrific resource for visiting privately owned gardens. Easily find out which gardens are open near your location from their website. A great way to meet local Cotswolds' residents and get a feel for a village if you are cottage hunting or to just visit beautifully presented gardens.

HIDCOTE MANOR GARDEN,

Near Chipping Camden, Gloucestershire, GL55 6LR

www.nationaltrust.org.uk

National Trust owned, was laid out over 70 years ago in a series of garden 'rooms'. Changes with the seasons and features sweeping views over the Vale of Evesham.

KIFSGATE COURT GARDEN,

Near Chipping Camden, Gloucestershire, GL55 6LN

www.kiftsgate.co.uk

Very close to Hidcote Gardens. Hardy garden fans can do both in one day. This one a must-see. A series of interconnecting gardens, part of which are terraced, offering spectacular views.

HIGHGROVE HOUSE GARDEN TOUR,
(Country home of Prince Charles)

Near Tetbury, Gloucestershire, GL8 8PH

www.highgrovegardens.com

A Thyme walk. Walled garden with climbing pear. Many garden rooms. Beautiful in June.

PAINSWICK ROCOCO GARDEN,

Painswick, Gloucestershire, GL6 6TH

www.rococogarden.org.uk

Anniversary Maze. Pigeon House. Kitchen garden. Red House and Pan, God of Love.

WESTONBERT ARBORETUM,
Tetbury, Gloucestershire, GL8 8Q5
www.forestry.gov.uk

16,000 trees within 17 miles of accessible paths and five national collections.

BATSFORD ARBORETUM,
Moreton-in-Marsh, Gloucestershire, GL56 9AB
www.batsarb.co.uk

Once home of the famous Mitford family. Deer park. Near Falconry Centre.

MANOR HOUSES

KELMSCOTT MANOR,
Near Lechlade, Oxfordshire, GL7 3HJ
www.kelmscottmanor.org.uk

Artist William Morris's country home looking just as it did when he lived there. Idyllic setting with gift shop selling his fabrics and artefacts and a small restaurant providing lunch or tea by the river. Only open two days a week in summer. Important to check opening times.

BUSCOT PARK,
Faringdon, Oxfordshire, SN7 8BU
www.buscot-park.com

National Trust owned Adam-style house dating from 1780 surrounded by 55-acre park, gardens and fabulous water gardens. Excellent collection of furniture and paintings. Includes painting of *The Sleeping Beauty* by Sir Edward Burne-Jones.

UPTON HOUSE,
Near Banbury, Oxfordshire, OX15 6HT
www.nationaltrust.org.uk

Smaller scale country home. Built in 1695. Filled with fine furniture and first class art. The garden alone is worth a visit, with a lawn that drops to terraced borders and pools.

CHASTLETON HOUSE,

Near Moreton-in-Marsh, Oxfordshire, GL56 0SU

www.nationaltrust.org.uk

National Trust owned Stuart manor. Built by Walter Jones. A step back in time to 1602, this house is noted for its Long Gallery which features an ornamented tunnel-vaulted ceiling.

CHAVENAGE HOUSE,

Near Tetbury, Gloucestershire, GL8 8XP

www.chavenage.com

Finest example of a Tudor mansion in Great Britain including furniture. Visited by Oliver Cromwell and haunted by Charles I and other ghosts.

SNOWSHILL MANOR,

Broadway, Gloucestershire, WR12 7JU

www.nationaltrust.org.uk

This National Trust property houses Charles Wade's eclectic collection of craftsmanship from all over the world. Charming organic garden.

OWLPEN MANOR,

Owlpen, Dursley, Gloucestershire, GL11 5BZ

www.owlpen.com

Romantic Tudor manor house rebuilt from original c.1200 by the Daunt family between 1464 and 1616. Largely untouched since then. Reputedly haunted by several benign ghosts.

RODMARTON MANOR,

Near Cirencester, Gloucestershire, GL7 6PF

www.rodmarton-manor.co.uk

A wonderful showcase for the Arts and Crafts movement. Furniture was especially made for the house. Elegant gardens surround the house.

WOODCHESTER MANSION,

Nr. Stroud, Gloucestershire, GL10 3TS

www.woodchestermansion.org.uk

A Grade I listed house in Victorian Gothic style. Unfinished but quality of the craftsmanship is excellent. Strange layout of house gives credence to its reputation of being haunted.

MINSTER LOVELL HALL,

Near Witney, Oxfordshire, OX29 0RN

www.english-heritage.org.uk

There has been a manor house on this site, on the banks of the Windrush River, since the 12th century, but the major part of the ruins here today are those of a large house built by William, Baron of Lovell in the 1430s after his return from the French wars.

PREHISTORIC SITES

ROLLRIGHT STONES,

Near Chipping Norton, Oxfordshire/Warwickshire border (See website for directions)

www.rollrightstones.co.uk

Neolithic ceremonial stone circles dating from 2500 BCE. Stone circles include: The King's Men, the King Stone and the Whispering Knights.

BELAS KNAP LONG BARROW,

Winchcombe, Gloucestershire
(See website for directions)

www.english-heritage.org.uk

Fine example of a Neolithic long barrow. This chambered tomb dates from 1400 BCE. Excavated in 1863. Artefacts from tomb are in the village folk museum in Winchcombe.

RAILWAY

GLOUCESTER AND WARWICKSHIRE RAILWAY,
Toddington, Gloucestershire, GL54 5DT

www.gwsr.com

Runs through the Cotswolds, Winchcombe, Cheltenham, Stow-in-the-Wold. Wonderful termini with huge old engines.

RESTAURANTS, PUBS and ACCOMMODATION

TROUT AT TADPOLE BRIDGE,
Faringdon, Oxfordshire, SN7 8RF

www.trout-inn.co.uk

On the Thames. In the Good Food Guide. Six bedrooms – six boat berths. Garden goes down to the Thames. Great food and atmosphere.

THE WOOLPACK,
Slad, Gloucestershire, GL6 7QA

www.thewoolpackinn-slad.com

Beautiful setting made famous by author Laurie Lee's *Cider with Rosie.* Pub only. Great food. Sunday barbeque at certain times.

THE SWAN INN,
Swinbrook, Oxfordshire, OX18 4DY

www.theswanswinbrook.co.uk

Fabulous old pictures of the famous Mitford Sisters family who lived nearby adorn this pub and inn. Rooms above. Great food. Chickens run free in the garden.

THE FOX AT ODDINGTON,
Near Moreton-in-Marsh, Gloucestershire, GL56 0UR

www.foxinn.net

Charming ancient inn with three bedrooms and really good food. Make sure to visit nearby St Nicholas Church to see the *Domesday* paintings. This is the older of two churches in Oddington.

THE TUNNEL HOUSE INN AND BARN,
Cirencester, Gloucestershire, GL7 6PW

www.tunnelhouse.com

Wonderfully atmospheric. Memorabilia. Good food. Barn can be hired for large parties. B&Bs in the area. Camping in the grounds. No rooms.

THE GREEDY GOOSE,
Chastleton, Gloucestershire, GL56 0SP

www.thegreedygoosemoreton.co.uk

Up to the minute, peppy. Serves a terrific Sunday roast, all the traditional British favourites and more besides. Elegant patio. Tasty varied food.

THE WINDMILL CARVERY,
Nr. Burford, Oxfordshire, OX18 4HJ

www.windmillcarvery.co.uk

Good food. Reasonable prices. Lovely view. Great for Sunday lunch. Stroll around historic Burford afterwards to walk off the large portions.

THE POTTING SHED PUB,
Crudwell, Malmesbury, Wiltshire, SN16 9EW

www.thepottingshedpub.com

Beautiful old pub. Beams. Roaring fire. Pub grows own veg in veg patch and garden of 2 acres. Good, fresh food. Beers on tap. No rooms. Accommodation nearby.

LE MANOIR AUX QUAT' SAISONS,
Great Milton, Oxfordshire, OX44 7PD

www.manoir.com

Raymond Blanc's restaurant and hotel. Only for those with very deep pockets. A little outside the Cotswolds. Food beyond sublime. Romantic setting. Rooms Versailles-inspired *haute décor.*

THE FALKLAND ARMS,
Great Tew, Chipping Norton, Oxfordshire, OX7 4DB

www.falklandarms.co.uk

Flagstone floors. Oak beams. Roaring fire. Garden. Beers on tap. Rooms with 4-poster beds.

THE SWAN at Southrop,

Southrop, Gloucestershire, GL7 3NU

www.theswanatsouthrop.co.uk

Beautiful early 17th century, wisteria-covered inn. Halcyon village in the Leach valley. Rooms in cottages on the exquisite Southrop Manor Estate. Top-notch, delicious food.

EDGEMOOR INN,

Near Painswick, Gloucestershire, GL6 6ND

www.edgemoor-inn.com

Spectacular views from terrace as inn overlooks entire Painswick valley and is situated on the Cotswold Way. Great food and beer. Close to Haresfield Beacon. No rooms.

ROMAN SETTLEMENTS

NORTH LEIGH ROMAN VILLA,

Witney, Oxfordshire, OX29 8ER

www.thecotswoldgateway.co.uk

Remains of Roman Villa with 60 rooms. Intact mosaic floor in stunning reds and browns.

CHEDWORTH ROMAN VILLA,

Yanworth, Cheltenham, Gloucestershire, GL54 3LJ

One of the finest Romano-British villas in Britain. Features 4th century mosaics. Bathhouses and a water shrine. Museum and on-going excavations.

VIEWS

HARESFIELD BEACON,

3 miles north west of Stroud (see website for directions)

www.gloucestershire.gov.uk

National Trust site on the Cotswold escarpment with spectacular views across to Wales. Site of a Roman-British hill fort.

DEVIL'S CHIMNEY,

Leckhampton Hill, Near Cheltenham, Gloucestershire
(See website for directions)

www.cheltenham4u.co.uk

A limestone rock formation that stands above a quarry. Named for its shape as it resembles a twisted chimney. A local landmark whose origins are not known. Wonderful views across Cheltenham.

CLEEVE HILL,

Near Cheltenham, Gloucestershire
(See website for directions)

www.cheltenham4u.co.uk

The highest point both in the Cotswolds and the county of Gloucestershire. Gorgeous views over Prestbury and the Cheltenham Racecourse. On a clear day it is possible to see the Severn Vale and the Malvern Hills

BROADWAY TOWER,

Middle Hill, Broadway, Worcestershire, WR12 7LB

www.broadwaytower.co.uk

Completed in 1798 this folly was built for Lady Coventry on a beacon hill. Spectacular views of more than a dozen counties. Over 17 metres high. Open to the public.

WEAVING

COTSWOLD WOOLLEN WEAVERS,

Filkins, Gloucestershire, GL7 3JJ

www.dspace.dial.pipex.com/town/plaza/hk67/

18th century working woollen mill manufactures cloth exactly as it did all those years ago. Watch it in operation then stroll around the ancient village of Filkins and visit its two churches or if you wish the Five Alls pub.

WILDLIFE

COTSWOLDS WILDLIFE PARK,
Near Burford, Oxfordshire, OX18 4JP
www.cotswoldwildlifepark.co.uk
Lions, zebras and many more species in 160 acres of parkland. Great day out with the kids.

COTSWOLD FALCONRY CENTRE,
Batsford Park, Moreton-in-Marsh, GL56 9QB
www.cotswold-falconry.co.uk
Huge variety of birds of prey. Flying shows. Falcon displays. Great for the kids, too.

Tourist Information Centres

There are 20 Tourist Information Centres throughout the Cotswolds. Access them through this web site:
www.the-cotswolds.org

COSTWOLDS TOURIST INFO

www.cotswolds.info
www.the-cotswolds.org

COTSWOLDS CONSERVATION BOARD

www.cotswoldsaonb.org.uk

The Cotswolds Conservation Board exists to conserve and enhance the Cotswolds Area of Outstanding Natural Beauty (AONB). Established in 2004, the board is the only organization to look after the AONB as a whole and is a statutory body created as a result of the Countryside and Rights Act (CROW) 2000.

The Cotswolds was designated an Area of Outstanding Natural Beauty in 1966 and extended in area in 1990. This designation is to ensure the conservation and enhancement of the natural beauty of the Cotswolds which covers 790 square miles.

SOCIETY FOR THE PROTECTION OF ANCIENT BUILDINGS

www.spab.org.uk

SPAB is a membership organization fighting to save historic and listed buildings from decay, demolition and destruction. Founded by William Morris, the artist, to fight the insensitive restoration of ancient buildings during the Victorian era and ongoing.

NATIONAL TRUST

www.nationaltrust.org.uk

Members pay no entrance fee for castles, stately homes, etc. Membership package takes 4 weeks to arrive.

COTSWOLD DRY STONE WALL CLASSES

www.thecotswoldgateway.co.uk

Learn how to build a dry stone wall – a declining art in the Cotswolds. Carry on the tradition.

COTSWOLDS FARMERS MARKETS AND FARMERS SHOPS

www.thecotswoldgateway.co.uk

COTSWOLDS FETES, EVENTS, COUNTY SHOWS ETC.

www.events.wiltsglosstandard.co.uk

Conservation in The Cotswolds: Dry Stone Wall Repair

INDEX

Printed by:

Copytech (UK) Limited trading as
Printondemand-worldwide,
9 Culley Court,
Bakewell Road,
Orton Southgate,
Peterborough,
PE2 6XD